Birds&Blooms

Birds in Every Season

Great blue heron, page 152

Table of Contents

ON THE FRONT COVER
Summer tanager
Photo by Kevan Sunderland, page 40

ON THE TITLE PAGE
Indigo bunting
Photo by Bob Quarles, page 74

Yellow warbler,
page 44

**Chief Content Officer,
Home & Garden** Jeanne Sidner

Content Director Mark Hagen

Creative Director
Raeann Thompson

Editor Julie Kuczynski

Senior Editor Julie Schnittka

Assistant Editor Sammi DiVito

Senior Art Director
Kristen Stecklein

Senior Designer Anna Jo Beck

Deputy Editor, Copy Desk
Dulcie Shoener

Copy Editor Kara Dennison

Contributing Editor
Jennifer Zeigler

A *Birds & Blooms* Book

ISBN:
978-1-62145-976-7 (Hardcover)
978-1-62145-977-4 (Paperback)
978-1-62145-985-9 (Epub)

Component Number:
118500122H

We are committed to both
the quality of our products
and the service we provide to
our customers. We value your
comments, so please feel free
to contact us at *TMBBookTeam@
TrustedMediaBrands.com.*

For more *Birds & Blooms* products
and information, visit our website:
www.birdsandblooms.com.

Hardcover printed in China
10 9 8 7 6 5 4 3 2 1

Paperback printed in China
10 9 8 7 6 5 4 3 2 1

Text, photography and illustrations
for *Birds in Every Season* are based
on articles previously published
in *Birds & Blooms* magazine
(*www.birdsandblooms.com*).

Blue jay, page 135

Welcome!

A chance sighting of a rare migrant or even photographing a daily feathered visitor can be exciting. Share in the joy with fellow *Birds & Blooms* readers who've spotted beautiful birds around the country. Seasonal backdrops make the images and stories even more vibrant. Plus, learn quick tips and read up on sound advice from our experts on birding at different times of the year in *Birds in Every Season*. Be it spring, summer, fall or winter—birdwatching is always in season!

—THE EDITORS OF
BIRDS & BLOOMS MAGAZINE

CHAPTER 1

Spring

As soon as the snow begins to melt, temperatures start climbing and days become longer. The arrival of feathered friends is eagerly anticipated.

Prothonotary warblers are one of my all-time favorite birds, and I was so excited to find a breeding pair along the Wisconsin River. I took a photo of the male delivering food to the babies inside the nest. I could hear their excited chirps inside the tree cavity, but it wasn't until I got home and checked the photo more closely that I realized you could see four hungry mouths inside the tree. It was such an amazing birding experience!

Andy Raupp MONTELLO, WISCONSIN

One spring,

I saw this black-and-white warbler while looking out my living room window. I grabbed my Nikon D5600 and ran outside, hoping to get a picture of the bird. This was the only shot that turned out.

Karen Fortney
LIVINGSTON, TEXAS

Our treehouse

has attracted a mating pair of eastern screech-owls for several years. This usually results in three or four owlets. They're born in March and fledge in early May. We watch them from our back patio—they're unbothered by our quiet presence. This photo is of the owlets when they learned to perch and view the big world outside. While almost full size already, they are still mostly covered with their owlet fuzz.

Dwayne Mann
WEST LAKE HILLS, TEXAS

Each spring,

we see a variety of birds flocking at our backyard feeders. Most of them use the nearby crabapple tree as a perch before and after feeding. One morning, I captured this male American goldfinch perched high in the treetop. The weather was very cool so he was all puffed up, trying to stay warm. It was a truly beautiful sight!

Craig Gemming
COLUMBIA, MISSOURI

PRACTICAL BEAUTY

Flowering trees such as dogwoods, crabapples or redbuds offer color and fruit for birds.

I've always found Baltimore

orioles to be skittish and very difficult to photograph. But my husband and I had good fortune one day and attracted this beauty by putting out some jelly. This particular bird had a real sweet beak. It didn't care that I was only a few feet away when I used my husband's Canon EOS 80D to take a photo.

Stephanie Red Feather
PLATTE CITY, MISSOURI

I often stop at Gilbert's Corner Regional Park in Virginia after work. Walking the trail is so cathartic after a long shift at the hospital. The wildflowers at the park offer an abundant buffet for the birds—they're usually busy gorging themselves and don't mind me. I love this photo of a song sparrow because of how it's perched between the two stalks.

Laura Frazier KEARNEYSVILLE, WEST VIRGINIA

A mourning dove posed in our pink dogwood tree one evening. It's a common bird with a very distinct call. Even though the low, sorrowful sound may seem melancholy, the mourning dove is considered to be a messenger of peace, faith and love.

Tim Deitz LANCASTER, OHIO

The loud song

of the Carolina wren is unmistakable. It drew me to the backyard, where I crept up slowly and positioned myself behind a pine tree. The wren perched in a dogwood tree, crooning noisily. I got some images thanks to my Nikon D500.

Louis Ruttkay
LANCASTER, PENNSYLVANIA

Mama called this wood duck

chick to jump out of the nest just one day after it hatched. I have three nest boxes, each with a security camera inside so I'll know when this event will happen—and I have my Nikon D7200 ready. The chicks had no flight feathers yet, so they bounced, rolled and plopped to the ground before joining their mom. It was adorable to watch.

Sue Clark
STUART, FLORIDA

A LEAP OF FAITH

Wood duck chicks can safely exit nests up to 70 feet in the air.

Flying low to the ground, an ash-throated flycatcher was foraging for insects in my backyard. These birds don't need to drink water, but instead get the moisture they need from insects. I sat on the ground for quite a while to capture this image with the bird at eye level, looking right at me. I took the photo with my Canon EOS70D and Sigma lens.

Stephanie Becker
MORAGA, CALIFORNIA

Spring arrived and my purple plum tree bloomed once again. The tree is right outside my breakfast nook window. I've spent many hours peering out that window, taking photos of all the lovely birds that came to visit, including this stunning male northern cardinal.

Jacqueline Hodsdon
FOREST, VIRGINIA

I spent countless hours watching and photographing wild birds in the backyard when we were all stuck at home because of COVID-19, and we really discovered the beauty of nature all around us. I used my Nikon D750 with a Tamron 100-400 mm lens braced on a tripod to capture this Carolina wren with loropetalum branches in the background.

Robert Faulks ABERDEEN, MISSISSIPPI

Evening grosbeaks grace our yard for much of the year, displaying their cheerful behaviors for all to enjoy. Our pond provides a quick drink and bathing spot where we can observe the birds in their flock. The reflections provide a one-of-a-kind look at this impressive bird.

Douglas Beall CAMP SHERMAN, OREGON

I had a wonderful

sighting at my former home in Murfreesboro, Tennessee. I had just filled the coffeepot when I saw this little male American kestrel perched on the awning framework. I had never seen one, and I just stood there—until my brain engaged and I made a mad dash for my camera. I snapped away in auto mode. The reflected sunlight from the 2-inch snow cover and the white siding of the house filled in the shadows quite nicely. I was getting ready to move, and it was a great going-away photo!

Jeff Shepard
RIO VISTA, CALIFORNIA

Mourning warblers

usually spend their time close to the forest floor. When I was at the Chippewa Nature Center in Midland, Michigan, this male ventured up a tall bush to ring out his beautiful song. (I took this picture with my Nikon D500 and Sigma 150-600 mm lens.) Seeing a mourning warbler in the open is a privilege because of the species' secretive nature.

Evan Reister
WILLIAMSBURG, MICHIGAN

During a visit to the nature center at Kensington Metropark in Michigan, I was told that some sandhill crane colts were nearby with their parents. I immediately went to them and started taking photos of the cute group. Upon seeing the pictures, my wife pointed out that one of the colts was indeed a gosling, not a crane. Many photographers also captured the crane family together through spring. The two crane partners lovingly raised the gosling as their own along with its colt sibling.

Ray Closson MARSHALL, MICHIGAN

This was the first time I had cedar waxwings in my yard. I love these birds and was pretty excited to have them visit. I photographed this one as it sat in a tree. The flock stayed in my area for several days. I adore their little high-pitched call.

Laura Johnson
CATHLAMET,
WASHINGTON

TWO-NOTE WONDERS
Cedar waxwing repertoire consists of a high, thin *bzeee* and a sighing whistle.

Devouring a hearty meal can sure be tiring! This house sparrow looks so peaceful nodding off after its meal. I understand. After all, who doesn't love a good after-dinner nap?

Katharine Wall
WESTMINSTER,
MASSACHUSETTS

The flowering plum trees bloomed early one year—just in time for the Townsend's warblers to sip their sweet nectar. I was there with my Nikon D5 to capture the moment.

Leslie Scopes Anderson ARCATA, CALIFORNIA

A family of robins moved in next to my front door one spring. I set up my Canon DSLR near the nest and used a long USB cord to connect it to my computer inside the house for remote shooting. I spent countless hours watching the birds on my screen and taking hundreds of pictures. I call this one *Peekaboo*.

Adam Fine LIVERPOOL, NEW YORK

I came upon

this gorgeous eastern kingbird as I was walking at the Arboretum at the University of Guelph in Ontario, Canada. It looked so pretty perched on a branch of crabapple blossoms.

Brenda Doherty
ARISS, ONTARIO

I've always loved birds,

but I just recently took up birding. I took this shot of a male scarlet tanager over Memorial Day weekend near my parents' log home in northern Michigan. He appeared for only about 15 seconds before disappearing into the woods. I used a Nikon D7000 and a Nikkor 200-500 mm lens to take the picture.

Victoria Martel
MUSKEGON, MICHIGAN

I love feeding

the birds in my yard and taking pictures of nature. I keep a journal logging the various birds that visit my home. This male red-bellied woodpecker is one of my favorites, along with the tiny hummingbirds that migrate to my area during spring.

Jennifer Davis
BEAR CREEK TOWNSHIP, PENNSYLVANIA

I couldn't believe my eyes

when I looked out my back window and saw this sight. Although cedar waxwings are yearlong residents here in eastern Tennessee, I rarely see them, let alone in massive flocks. But I watched this large group land in a nearby tree and then, all at once, fly to the birdbath. Imagine the surprise of this robin— bathing quietly one moment, swarmed by waxwings the next! It kept bathing, however, and didn't seem to mind.

Elise Blosser
KNOXVILLE, TENNESSEE

I was amazed when I went for a walk and spotted this small chickadee perched in a forsythia bush that was just starting to bloom. It was truly a beautiful "birds and blooms" sight.

Pat Shaw WARREN, MICHIGAN

The redbud tree in my backyard is the first to bloom and announce that spring is on the way. This tree is very special because it moved with me from Oklahoma to Texas decades ago. Since that time, it has grown from a sapling into a mature tree. I look forward to seeing its beautiful light pink blossoms and photographing the birds that perch there, such as this tufted titmouse.

Cynthia Lockwood THE WOODLANDS, TEXAS

Goldfinches are the birds

that initially made me fall in love with birdwatching. I snapped a photo of this male when it stopped in my backyard.

Sara Wunderlich
FOLEY, MINNESOTA

My husband

and I vacationed in Arizona, visiting the Grand Canyon, Sedona and Scottsdale, and the beauty of the scenery and wildlife simply took our breath away. One morning, while photographing flowers and cactuses, I noticed this curious cactus wren watching me. As I looked closer, I saw that it was holding a fragment of plant material, probably for its nest.

These are usually vocal birds, but this one was quiet, patiently posing on a cactus branch for me to take a photo. Once I had my snapshot, it flew away.

Cristina Martinez
TORONTO, ONTARIO

I spotted a male house finch sitting in the cherry tree outside my home. I waited patiently until he posed regally for me. I captured the photo using a Nikon Coolpix B700 at the full focal length.

Maureen Dwyer
HAVERFORD, PENNSYLVANIA

I always look forward to the spring warbler migration. A pond across the street from our house attracts several types of warblers every year. I was especially thrilled to see a set of three Canada warblers over the course of five days. This one posed for me for a few minutes.

Elisa Shaw
RED HOOK, NEW YORK

The blue jays that visit our feeders are difficult to photograph. They're very skittish, darting in to snatch a peanut and then quickly flying away to either enjoy it or stash it for later. Oftentimes, the greedy jays store one peanut in their craw before plucking a second one and flying away. This photo captures the blue jay's personality in a nutshell as well as the sparkle in its eye. I used a Canon EOS 7D Mark II with a 100-400 mm zoom lens to take the shot.

Linda Taylor WACO, TEXAS

I saw these three young pileated woodpeckers at Brazos Bend State Park in Texas one spring. They stuck their heads out of the tree, waiting for their mother to feed them. I caught this moment using my Nikon D700 camera and a Sigma 150-500 mm telephoto lens.

Jeffrey Zwiers KATY, TEXAS

Each spring, cardinals and house finches pull the blossoms off my purple leaf plum tree. It's a sight to see. They don't really eat the flowers—they just let them fall to the ground. The tree is right outside my breakfast nook, so this gives me a chance to get some delightful photos.

Jacqueline Hodsdon FOREST, VIRGINIA

White-throated sparrows forage in dark leaf litter, so it's difficult to get a nice photo of them. I got lucky one spring day at Huntley Meadows Park near Alexandria, Virginia, when this individual stopped to eat its lunch. Perhaps it needed a napkin to clean up afterward!

Jody Partin
OCEANSIDE, CALIFORNIA

This was just a sweet moment.

A Carolina wren visits our backyard often. I love the way the bird sits on the little boy's knee. I took this photo with a Sony a6000.

Carmella Poole
GRETNA, LOUISIANA

This mourning dove was certainly comfortable and content perching in my backyard. It let me get close as it preened and ruffled its feathers.

Martin Torres
PORT HURON, MICHIGAN

STAYING TIDY
Birds preen to adjust the way their barbules, tiny strands of feathers, interlock. This maintains their water-resistant coat.

Springtime is exciting after a long, cold Ohio winter. Migrants are in their best colors, especially the males, and getting some nice shots is my goal. The blue-gray gnatcatcher is especially sought after—getting a photo of one is a bit challenging, so I was happy to capture this.

Debbie Parker
HEFFIELD VILLAGE, OHIO

During the first few weeks of the pandemic, I took this photo.
A trumpeter swan with babies on its back swam near me and then walked up to
say hello. The two babies waddled onto shore and started snuggling. Everything
in the world seemed so bleak at the time, and this photo reminds me that nature
always finds a way to keep going and bring in new life. I used a Panasonic Lumix
DC-G9 camera with a 100-400 mm lens.

Marlon Porter MISSISSAUGA, ONTARIO

This bird was my sunshine. I spotted it at the start of spring migration one year while driving on back roads. It was my first yellow warbler of the season.

Trisha Snider ST. THOMAS, ONTARIO

For two years, palm warblers landed in the same Norway spruces about 15 feet from my patio. I feel so lucky because I had never seen this bird before!

Trish Overton
EVANSVILLE, INDIANA

Every once in a while, a pileated woodpecker lands on a tree in my backyard. They're my absolute favorite—their bold red crests are so beautiful.

Raven Ouellette
SUDBURY, ONTARIO

CLOSE TO HOME
Though usually found in mature woods, pileated woodpeckers can also be drawn to yards with suet, diseased or dead trees, and empty nest boxes.

An eastern phoebe visited my backyard from winter through spring. It was the first time I had seen one stop by. The phoebe loved the peanut butter suet, and I enjoyed watching it wag its tail up and down as it perched on tree limbs.

Marie Lehmann
MILTON, FLORIDA

One morning, I heard a lovely song coming from my yard. I was stunned to see a flurry of warblers. Two of the birds had orange throats, which stopped me in my tracks. Over the years, I've traveled across New England visiting warbler hot spots in hopes of viewing a Blackburnian warbler. And to my utter shock, two were in my own yard! After shooting hundreds of photos that morning, I had a pretty severe case of warbler neck, but it was totally worth it.

Amy Severino
NEW IPSWICH,
NEW HAMPSHIRE

I had recently moved to my current home outside of the city limits when I took this photo. My new backyard is full of mature trees and, of course, many birds. I had never seen an indigo bunting in person until they started passing through this yard.

Amanda Piver HENDERSONVILLE, TENNESSEE

During spring migration, many summer tanagers make a long flight across the Gulf of Mexico. On this particular day, a weather front passed through South Texas, causing these migrating songbirds to struggle against a headwind to reach land. When the weather finally cleared by the afternoon, I knew the birds would land out of exhaustion. I drove around and found this amazing tanager on a bottlebrush tree. I was glad to see the bird had made the crossing.

Kevan Sunderland SUNRISE, ALBERTA

Living near a canal, I see ducks making their way through my backyard fairly often. One winter, a pair of mallards would appear and knock on the sliding glass door for food! In the spring, one of the ducks came with its ducklings and huddled to rest on the patio. Simply adorable!

Elizabeth Kiester
MCCALL, IDAHO

One of my favorite migrating birds is the beautiful rose-breasted grosbeak. I was pleased to have a large number of males and females in my yard one spring. My doublefile viburnum was a large attraction for them and made a perfect backdrop.

Jean Owens
PARIS, TENNESSEE

I noticed some crabapple trees standing near a bluebird house in Chanhassen, Minnesota. I set up nearby and waited for this male eastern bluebird to stop at the tree before heading to his house. I captured him just as he was landing on this branch full of blooms. I was really happy to get a photo of this bird with his spring plumage in a beautiful tree.

Roslynn Long
BURNSVILLE, MINNESOTA

Much to my surprise, while hiking Buckeye Woods Park in Medina, Ohio, I stumbled across this black-throated blue warbler foraging. It was scanning the lush forest floor for insects and other goodies.

Debora Parker
MEDINA, OHIO

I captured this shot of a great egret with a Panasonic Lumix G85 while visiting some friends in Florida. I never realized how large and beautiful these birds are until I saw one in person. The experience was just wonderful!

Lance Bruce ZEBULON, NORTH CAROLINA

FIND THEM!
Warblers don't generally visit feeders. Draw them in with water features or go to a local migration hot spot. They tend to visit wet or elevated areas.

It was a happy and unexpected
surprise to have a yellow warbler visit our flowering pear tree. The bird arrived on an unseasonably cold morning in early May. Its little body was puffed out for warmth and its head was lifted skyward, which made it look all the more sweet. I took the image with a Nikon Coolpix P900 through a window while standing in the middle of our family room.

Pat Shaw WARREN, MICHIGAN

I took this picture of a majestic blue jay in spring. He was proudly perched outside the window of my sunroom. This handsome bird was special to me because it came nearly every day. To get this shot, I waited for him with my Nikon D5500 and 70-300 mm lens.

Lanis Rossi VOORHEES, NEW JERSEY

Spring brings lots of birds

to our yard. My favorite is the great crested flycatcher. It stays around Ohio for most of the summer before journeying south for the winter.

Debora Parker
MEDINA, OHIO

A bird perched

in a flowering tree is my idea of the perfect photo. Driving around the corner into a city park, I saw this northern mockingbird. I stopped for a few moments, left the car and snapped this picture. To me it almost looks like a bridal portrait.

Aneeta Brown
WASHINGTON, MISSOURI

I went camping at Garner State Park in Texas with my wife and stepson. Saturday afternoon was windy but beautiful, and suddenly this vermilion flycatcher appeared. Looking through the binocular lens, I couldn't believe my eyes. What a stunning bird!

Joseph Mandy
AUSTIN, TEXAS

I photographed this common yellowthroat in the spring with a Nikon D100. I love warblers and I am collecting photos of them singing. I spotted this one at Hoffman Hills State Recreation Area in Menomonie, Wisconsin.

Nina Koch
MENOMONIE, WISCONSIN

My wife planted succulents in a wooden planter in spring. We had a bird feeder less than 2 feet away, which got the attention of many, many American goldfinches. I set my Nikon D300S on a tripod with a wireless remote trigger and baited the birds by sprinkling some sunflower seeds on the succulents.

Jim Dickson ALBANY, OREGON

While I was sitting in my car at a park, this cool eastern kingbird swooped down and posed for me. It really made my day.

George Dokes WHITE HALL, ARKANSAS

This tree was planted for the shade but, much to my delight, cedar waxwings visit it every spring. They let me take photos while I sit on the patio. I captured this with a Sony a6000. I enjoy the photo for its subject and the effect of the blurred green leaves.

Pearl Bouchard
SPOKANE, WASHINGTON

I was visiting my mother's house and observing the birds fluttering around her feeder when I spotted this yellow-rumped warbler perched on a branch. It was posing perfectly for me. In the last couple of years, I've seen these warblers only at this location, so it was delightful to have an opportunity to photograph such an interesting bird.

Mark Ruppert
FREEPORT, MAINE

We had Cape May warblers foraging for nectar in our crabapple tree. You can see the pollen on this one's beak! These birds don't nest in our area. They're just passing through on their migration to northern breeding grounds.

Greg DuBois
JOLIET, ILLINOIS

Many of the mailboxes in my neighborhood have birdhouses attached to the posts. Every spring, the primary residents of these birdhouses are tree swallows, which are very protective of their houses and the nests inside. They'll even divebomb you if you get too close. I really wonder just how my neighbors get their mail out!

Jacqueline Hodsdon
FOREST, VIRGINIA

One spring, a few eastern bluebirds caught my eye in Clayton, Wisconsin. This adult was bringing food for its babies in the birdhouse.

PD Strickland CUMBERLAND, WISCONSIN

A LITTLE POP OF COLOR
Common yellowthroats get their name from the yellow patch running all the way from the base of their beak to their chest.

From what I've seen, most common yellowthroats usually like to hide, but not this one! It seemed especially curious and didn't disappear into the tall grass.

Laura Frazier KEARNEYSVILLE, WEST VIRGINIA

Green Cay Wetlands

in Boynton Beach, Florida, is a public nature center where visitors can see and photograph a variety of waterfowl and wading birds. When I visit my mother in South Florida, we spend a couple of days at Green Cay. On this particular trip, several roseate spoonbills were perched at the top of a dead tree—not where I expected to see them. The contrast of their red plumage against the bright sky was superb.

David Kassel
NAPA, CALIFORNIA

One of my favorite places

for birding is the Allyn Cox Reservation in Essex, Massachusetts. The trees burst with blossoms in April and May, luring the birds into their branches in search of insects and nectar. I found this Baltimore oriole there and watched as he hopped from branch to branch, pausing only briefly between bites.

Kathy Diamontopoulos
HAVERHILL, MASSACHUSETTS

This tree swallow set up its home in our backyard. At dusk, swallows are all over the yard, flying by and catching bugs. I took this photo with my Canon EOS 6D Mark II.

Debbie Clark
DECATUR, TENNESSEE

Sandhill cranes may seem somewhat awkward on land, but they often become graceful in flight. This crane was just one of hundreds I saw along the Platte River south of Grand Island, Nebraska.

Conda Allen
GRAND ISLAND,
NEBRASKA

MIGRATION MAGIC
Sandhill cranes move and spend winter in large groups. They are sometimes spotted in the thousands.

The spotted towhee inhabits many areas of western North America. The species tends to prefer forest edges, thickets and shrubby park areas. I took this photo while hiking along a trail near Boulder, Colorado. The towhee is sitting on a wild plum tree, which blooms in the foothills during spring. I was able to catch them both together.

Neal Zaun BOULDER, COLORADO

Home Tweet Home

From simple scrapes on the ground to elaborately woven structures, birds' nests are temporary yet meticulously built places to raise young. Learn about different housing styles and where various species choose to set up house.

By Ken Keffer

Power Nesting

It is hard to say officially *whoooo* lays the first eggs each year, but my pick for favorite nest is the great horned owl's. Sure, many species can begin nesting in January in southern states, but it is still winter in the northern states when great horned owls start incubating their eggs in nests made of sticks, often in trees. It's essential that these owls get an early start on nesting because the species is slow to hatch and fledge. It is remarkable to think of the owls sitting on eggs as snow piles up during frigid nights.

Great horned owls reuse nests made by hawks, eagles or crows.

Instead of building nests, thick-billed murres lay eggs on narrow ledges of steep cliffs.

Precarious Cliff Sides

Huge colonies of murres and guillemots nest on rocky coastal cliffs. Most lack any structural nests, instead laying eggs that are extra pointy on one end. This shape helps the eggs pivot around the point instead of rolling over the edge. These ledge nesting sites are also more protected from predators. Cliff nesters aren't found only on coasts. Lots of species, including condors, ravens and falcons, use cliffs, but they build stick nests in the crevices.

Killdeer lay eggs directly on the ground.

No Fuss

It's the exception rather than the rule, but a few species of birds get away with building hardly any nest at all. This doesn't mean they are haphazard in their approach to laying eggs, though. Beach nesting birds—including black skimmers, many species of terns, and piping, Wilson's and other plovers—lay eggs in shallow depressions scraped out in the sand. The remarkable thing about the eggs of these species is their cryptic camouflage coloration. Eggs are often speckled and match the sandy granules of the makeshift nests. Sometimes these birds will line the shallow scrape with shells or sand to add to the camouflage. As beaches get more developed, some of these beach nesters have adapted to laying eggs on nearby rooftops.

Intricate and Elaborate

Orioles are the seamstresses of the bird world. Their iconic pendant nests dangle from outermost tree branches. The nests are impossible to miss among the barren winter branches and nearly as impossible to spot, surrounded by leaves, during the breeding season. Orioles use whatever material is available to stitch their bag nests—long grasses, twine, or even horsehair. The nests are lined with soft materials such as plant fibers, feathers or animal wool. The Altamira oriole of extreme south Texas and Central America constructs one of the longest dangling nests, which can hang down more than 2 feet.

It might take a female Altamira oriole three weeks to build a nest, which can be 2 feet long.

Eagles' nests are made of sticks with soft materials, such as grass, moss and cornstalks, stuffed into the cracks.

ROLF NUSSBAUMER

Built to Last

The grand champion nest-builder is the bald eagle! In 1963, an eagle's nest near St. Petersburg, Florida, was declared the largest at nearly 10 feet wide, 20 feet deep and over 4,400 pounds. That nest was extreme; most bald eagle nests are 5 to 6 feet in diameter and 2 to 4 feet tall. Nest construction can take three months. Eagles typically use the same nest year after year, adding to it each season.

Small and Flexible

It should come as no surprise that hummingbirds, our smallest birds, make the smallest nests. Hummingbirds build on top of tree branches, using plants, soft materials and spider webs. Ruby-throats decorate theirs with flakes of lichen. Anna's hummingbirds may lay eggs before a nest is completed, continuing to build the sidewalls during incubation. Most impressive is how these nests stretch. Hummingbirds usually lay a pair of eggs the size of black beans inside a nest about the diameter of a quarter. As the babies grow, the nest expands, keeping things tight and cozy.

Once the eggs hatch, this hummingbird nest will stretch to accommodate the growing nestlings.

Bird Anywhere, Anytime

Start urban wildlife–watching with advice from acclaimed author and naturalist David Lindo.

By Kelsey Roseth

See surprising birds in the city, such as this cormorant in Elliott Bay near Seattle, Washington.

Brown pelicans fly over the Golden Gate Bridge in San Francisco, California.

T**HERE'S A MASSIVE MISCONCEPTION** about birding in urban areas.
Some assume it requires a depth of knowledge, awareness and skill to spot interesting birds in the city—but, in actuality, it couldn't be easier. According to David Lindo, who is internationally known as The Urban Birder, you start by simply looking up.

"It's amazing what you can see when you look up: swirling swifts, migrating thrushes, raucous crows, birds of prey. It's a beautiful world up there," David says.

An ever-curious naturalist, David was born in North West London and was enchanted by the outdoors at an early age.

"When I was about 3 years old, I went missing during a family party and caused my mum great panic. The police were called, a search party was dispatched, and I was eventually found standing outside a graveyard watching some magpies," David says. Now he's one of the leaders in the movement to observe nature in populated places.

With limited access to the English countryside, he started seeking feathered friends in the only place he could: around his bustling neighborhood. At 8 years old, he borrowed a field guide from the library and set out to study the scientific names, sizes and markings of all the local species. David became a notable local birding hobbyist. And in the early 2000s, his personal passion transformed into a budding career as a naturalist with a call from the British Broadcasting Corp. The BBC asked him to appear on the annual TV series *Springwatch*.

"I paced up and down the kitchen, thinking, *What I can say and do during my screen test?*" David says. "I wanted to be the next David Attenborough. I wanted to be out there clambering over rocks in the Galapagos and through jungles in Peru."

David Lindo

With time, his career began to blossom and he was birding worldwide, often visiting Los Angeles, New York City and Cleveland, among other cities. Now a broadcaster, writer, photographer, public speaker and tour operator, David is still encouraging everyone to set their eyes to the skies wherever they may be. Here's his best advice.

Keep It Simple
Whether you're sitting in a coffee shop, reading in a local park or commuting to work, try to awaken your senses. David says not to worry about having the best gear, guidebooks, binoculars and the rest. Once you open your mind and your eyes, you'll start seeing birds.

Pop Over to a Patch
In birding slang, a patch is a local area that's frequented by bird-watchers. "Don't be forced

Pigeons preen on a rooftop.

into feeling that you need to be an expert in five minutes—you need to do it at your pace," says David, who taught himself the basics of birding.

Set Your Own Rhythm

While there are those who seek to add as many species as possible to their life list, David recommends starting small. Cast the expectations, ditch the list, release the nagging pressure and simply observe. "I'm interested in being able to remember the experience by watching the bird and really studying it—and that, for me, is most exciting," he says.

Manage the Mindset

David's philosophy for watching wildlife revolves around seeing the world as birds would. "The buildings are cliffs, and any other green areas are an oasis for nesting, resting and feeding. Don't stress about learning the names and songs of all the birds you encounter; just enjoy them," he said.

Get Grounded

Bird-watching can be a spiritual experience for some. If you approach it with the right attitude, you'll soon discover that birds are just about everywhere.

"What excites me most about birding is the way it makes me feel when I'm doing it," David says. "I feel so at peace. Even when you might have problems, or during these troubled times, it's one of the few times you can have an escape. And it's good for you."

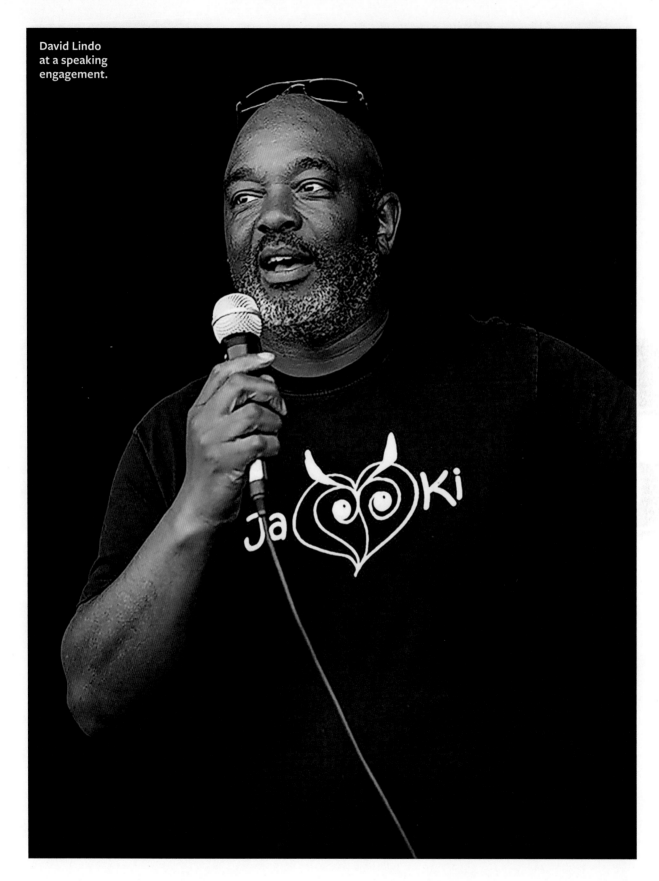

David Lindo
at a speaking
engagement.

CHAPTER 2

Summer

A nesting neighbor or two may be soaking up the sun in a backyard or a local green space during the summertime. Make sure to have a camera at the ready for a quick shot!

I kept seeing

a male blue grosbeak visit the red hot pokers just outside my dining room window, but each time I tried to go outside to catch a photo, he'd fly away. My wonderful husband, Tim, took out the window's screen so I could sit indoors and snap pictures of the bird eating from the flowers only several feet away. This worked brilliantly, and I was finally able to capture many photos. I love the contrast of his sapphire blue and rusty coloring against the bright flowers.

Laurie Stuchlik
MILTON, DELAWARE

Catbirds love

a cooling bath in my backyard during the heat of summer, and my wife enjoys mimicking their calls and trying to communicate with them. I photographed this scene with my Sony a5000 camera.

Courtney Rocheleau
SOMERSWORTH,
NEW HAMPSHIRE

Hello, friend! Curiosity got the better of this piping plover chick—it couldn't resist investigating a crustacean. Piping plovers return to our coastlines in early spring to nest and have young ones by June, my favorite time of year. Luckily, I live close by and am able to visit the beach to photograph the antics of these adorable little balls of fluff as they wander along the sand.

Kathy Diamontopoulos HAVERHILL, MASSACHUSETTS

After getting up early to beat the summer heat, I drove to a sunflower farm in Autaugaville, Alabama, where I saw an indigo bunting. I took this photo with a Nikon D850 full-frame camera on a tripod. If you look closely, you can see not only the beautiful bunting but also bees humming around the sunflower.

Bob Quarles BIRMINGHAM, ALABAMA

While visiting my in-laws

in Arizona, I enjoyed seeing the many different species of birds that thrive in the Southwest. The gorget on this male Anna's hummingbird added an intense pop of color to an otherwise monochromatic scene.

Mark Pope
SARASOTA, FLORIDA

Goldfinches love zinnia

seeds and often visit my little patch of blooms. They tend to prefer the older zinnias' ripe seeds, so I was very happy to get a picture of a male with some of the prettier flowers.

Jackie Latham
COLUMBUS, GEORGIA

My neighbor

asked me to pick his tomatoes while he was out of town. I was surprised to see this young northern mockingbird perched on the tomato cage. It seemed a little grumpy to see me!

Angela Polen
FLORENCE,
SOUTH CAROLINA

VENTURING OUT A BIT

If you see a fledgling—a baby bird fully covered in feathers—away from its nest, don't be alarmed. It's likely exploring, and typically a parent is nearby.

While visiting

Swan Lake Iris Gardens in Sumter, South Carolina, I was very interested in the lighting on this mute swan. As the swan was preening, its head went below its raised wing and was shadowed by the sunlit wing feathers.

Joel Singletary
DALZELL,
SOUTH CAROLINA

Bells Bend Park in Nashville, Tennessee, has bountiful opportunities for viewing wildlife. While on an early morning summer walk, I observed some incredible bird activity. A male blue grosbeak with an insect let out repeated metallic calls, alarming his neighbors. An orchard oriole pair came to investigate the disturbance. Just as the three birds landed on the same stalk, I captured this image with my Nikon D500 camera and a Sigma 150-600 mm lens. Being in the right place at the right time to witness this feather frenzy was truly a magical moment and one that I will always remember.

Mary Glynn Williamson NASHVILLE, TENNESSEE

This juvenile robin had an adorable expression on its face while singing its little heart out. It's as if the youngster was saying "Here I am, world!" I took the photo in 2020, and observing this sweet bird brought a few moments of peace and comfort during a difficult and uncertain time.

Abbye Harlow DOLGEVILLE, NEW YORK

My backyard feeder attracts all kinds of beautiful birds, and on this day, an indigo bunting and a house finch decided to share a meal.

Michael DeLong
WAUWATOSA, WISCONSIN

FEED THE MASSES
Reach out to a nearby bird-feeding specialty store for top tips on welcoming both year-round local visitors and migratory ones.

A great horned owl was born in a nest built by a red-tailed hawk family a few years ago. I didn't know the young owl was there until I looked up and saw its little head. The owls have never been too afraid of me, but I guess it's because they grew up listening to me talk. The young owl stays around our yard being a little showoff, and I love it. I captured this photograph with a Nikon D50 camera.

Lynn Deeg
AMERICAN FALLS, IDAHO

I was taking photos of my daughter in a field when an indigo bunting landed not too far away. Nothing says summer like sunflowers and buntings together.

Heather Russell
WHITSETT,
NORTH CAROLINA

Brown pelicans nearly disappeared from the Gulf Coast several decades ago because of pesticide use. Though they were listed as an endangered species from 1970 until 2009, it's now easy to spot these pelicans, largely thanks to the 1972 ban on DDT. During the spring and summer, as boaters head south to Horn Island and other barrier islands that the National Park Service manage, the birds are a welcome sight. It's as if the pelicans are telling everyone to have fun and be safe.

Cindee Skelton
GAUTIER, MISSISSIPPI

I consider myself a true bluebird landlord after five years of hosting a mated pair of bluebirds. They stay in the backyard year-round and raise three broods every year. Most of their offspring stay in my yard until the following spring, when they set out to find their own territory. I like to feed them live mealworms from decorative bowls that I find at thrift shops. When I took this picture, my first thought was that it resembles me when I'm given a bowl of ice cream!

Rebecca Boyd KNOXVILLE, TENNESSEE

While photographing wild birds

in Arizona, I found this male ladder-backed woodpecker hunting for bugs on a dead branch. Suddenly, a male pyrrhuloxia landed on the same branch. Each seemed surprised to see the other there. After a brief standoff, the pyrrhuloxia flew away.

Kelly Walkotten HUDSONVILLE, MICHIGAN

DESERT WILDLIFE
The Arizona-Sonora Desert Museum hosts a variety of birds, including Anna's hummingbirds, cactus wrens and elf owls.

This shot was taken during a hot summer day at the Arizona-Sonora Desert Museum in Tucson. I had never seen a female varied bunting eat from a cactus fruit, so it was very exciting for me to snap this moment.

Dawn Arjes PAW PAW, ILLINOIS

I must have spent an hour snapping dozens and dozens of pictures of green jays while visiting the Rio Grande Valley in southern Texas. This photo stood out because of the seed the bird is about to snap up.

Sara Danta
CAMBRIA, CALIFORNIA

HEAD SOUTH
To spot a green jay in the U.S., you'll need to travel to southern Texas.

The head tilt of this male house finch was too adorable to not capture in a photo. It was a sunny summer day in New York and the little guy was waiting for the bird feeder to be filled—I guess I was taking too long. I used a Nikon Coolpix P1000 camera for the shot.

Gail DeAngelo
SCHENECTADY, NEW YORK

While at the

Botany Bay Plantation Wildlife Management Area on Edisto Island, South Carolina, during the summer, I was so excited to capture this image of a male painted bunting on a sunflower. I used a Sony Alpha 9 camera with a Sony 200-600 mm lens.

Rhonda Epper
MOUNT PLEASANT, SOUTH CAROLINA

VIVID BEAUTY

Though male painted buntings (left) certainly pop, keep an eye out for the bright yellow-green females, which also stand out among North American birds.

Herons perch

perfectly still or wade slowly through shallow water when fishing, making them easy to photograph. But I was struck by the pose of this green heron and wondered what it could see through the green algae on top of the water. It stayed that way for quite some time before resuming a more relaxed stance and flying off.

David Baxter
NORTH CANTON, OHIO

We placed this feeder right outside our window so that our two indoor cats could enjoy it along with us. These two male downy woodpeckers have been frequent visitors. That's Papa, on the left, teaching Junior all about suet feeders.

Gaye Benson COBBLE HILL, BRITISH COLUMBIA

I came across this male blue grosbeak and his mate at a trailhead near Golden, Colorado, one July morning. I was delighted that the two allowed me to enter their world as they danced around mullein blooms. The male perched atop this particular mullein and stood for a couple of frames. For a moment he acknowledged my presence in a sort of yoga pose, which I decided to call the downward grosbeak.

Brian Sump GOLDEN, COLORADO

Wild cardinal flowers were growing along the stream where I snapped this photo. I was attempting to get photographs of dragonflies but was pleasantly surprised to see a female ruby-throated hummingbird at the blooms.

Anne Donovan Fortier
BANGOR, MAINE

My husband and I visited Mount Lemmon near Tucson, Arizona, one July. High up on the mountain, the temperature was cool and quite refreshing. I saw several new-to-me bird species, but the yellow-eyed juncos were especially fun to watch! I love their rusty colors, yellow eyes and the expressive looks they gave me while they munched away on bugs.

Renee Frederick
LOGAN, OHIO

During one fall migration, I saw six different warblers, but my favorite was this beautiful male black-throated blue warbler. I feel very fortunate to have snapped this photo, since warblers never seem to stand still for long.

Nancy Tully
EAST STROUDSBURG,
PENNSYLVANIA

I waited most of the summer to snap a photo of these cardinals together in front of the flag, though I never thought I would capture such a perfect picture. I'm no professional, but photos like this make me interested in learning more about photography. I purchased a Nikon D5600 and plan to practice more.

Nina McMasters
TUNNELTON,
WEST VIRGINIA

While I was birding with my granddaughter in late July at Killdeer Plains, a local wildlife area in central Ohio, she told me to stop the car and back up. Posing and singing for us nearly within arm's reach of the car was this lovely male dickcissel. Not 10 minutes earlier we had almost given up birding for the day because it had rained.

Laura Marshall PROSPECT, OHIO

From my kitchen window, I saw a bit of yellow in the Bahama strongbark, an endangered Florida native tree, in my backyard. So I quickly grabbed my camera, went out to the front yard and circled around the back to not disturb what I thought for sure must be a bird. Thankfully, this juvenile spot-breasted oriole was still there, enjoying the tree's berries.

Phoenix SpiritDiva MIAMI, FLORIDA

While on a vacation in Indian Rocks Beach, Florida, we stayed at a motel right next to a skimmer nesting area. I enjoyed just sitting and watching them for hours.

Kathryn Herndon
FLORAL CITY, FLORIDA

I was visiting my children in New England and rented a condo in the woods. I laid out some seed on the balcony and had a steady stream of visitors almost immediately! This little black-capped chickadee took its time picking out the very best morsel to eat.

Caroline Brown
BONITA SPRINGS, FLORIDA

SERVE UP SEED
Black-capped chickadees love sunflower seeds! They peck a hole in the shell to pick out the tiny bits of seed.

I love watching hummingbirds.
During the summer this beautiful leucistic hummingbird visited my cleome when the other hummingbirds wouldn't share the feeders.

Louise Devore HUNTINGTON, WEST VIRGINIA

WEARING WHITE

Leucistic birds, such as this hummingbird, have a genetic condition that reduces the amount of pigment in their feathers.

Late in the summer, a female prairie warbler lived in our garden for several days. She ate bugs and flitted around, giving us endless entertainment. Early one evening she took a long and very enthusiastic bath in our little fountain, becoming soaked and looking quite comical! She spent about 10 minutes splashing around, having a great time.

Deborah Bifulco NEWTON, NEW JERSEY

One summer

I visited Linville Falls National Park, on the Blue Ridge Parkway, where I found this male black-throated blue warbler singing his heart out.

David Bell
CARY, NORTH CAROLINA

A three-hour wait

resulted in this shot of a female rufous pursuing an insect. It happened in the blink of an eye. It's interesting that hummingbirds eat insects for protein and fat—nectar isn't their only source of food.

Jack Moskovita
TACOMA, WASHINGTON

While all hummingbirds

are capable of midair contortions, I've found none more acrobatic than the black-chinned species. In this photo, I like how the prickly pear cactus flower provides a way to show the bird's diminutive size. And the bird's yellow-dusted bill reminds us that hummingbirds play an important role in the pollination process.

Greg Tucker
LOS ANGELES, CALIFORNIA

It makes me happy

when eastern bluebird parents bring their fledglings to my feeders, knowing that they will be well fed with plenty of mealworms and sunflower chips. I took this with a Nikon D500 and a Sigma 150-600 mm Contemporary lens a few weeks after the second brood fledged.

Kathy S. Brumbelow
MARIETTA, GEORGIA

When visiting the Animal Kingdom at Florida's Walt Disney World, the grandkids and I sat next to a river to eat. This great blue heron, looking for lunch, took a piece of bread that fell from our table. To my surprise, instead of eating it, the bird started fishing with it, putting the morsel in the water for bait—and it caught a fish! What an amazing thing to witness.

Eugene McQuillan FORT WAYNE, INDIANA

I love orioles, and they love the red hot poker plants in my backyard. This male Bullock's oriole was feeding on the blooms. The plants have sturdy stems that are strong enough to support a bird's weight. As many as four orioles feed simultaneously on my poker patch. I hope more people will plant this spectacular flower for this beautiful bird!

Marina Schultz FRUITA, COLORADO

Taken in my yard one summer with a Canon EOS 5D Mark III, this blue jay image stands out as one of my best. I was shooting birds in flight when this jay leaned forward. I was expecting it to take off, but it turned out that the jay was just waiting to have dinner delivered.

Deborah Morrison
BOWERSTON, OHIO

We often take
our daughter
to visit a small zoo in nearby Bear Hollow Park. On one trip I spied my favorite songbird, a golden-crowned kinglet, nervously hopping from limb to limb. Because it's so active, this kinglet is one of the hardest to photograph. I took a series of pictures, and this is my best. I like the way it shows off the bird's expression. After photographing more than 180 bird species, I still find it thrilling to capture a bird's personality in a snapshot.

Brandon Adams
COMER, GEORGIA

SIMILAR SPRITES
Golden-crowned kinglets are nearly as tiny as hummingbirds, and just as active.

While I was taking photos of my sunflowers, this little ruby-throated hummingbird flew up and perched on a leaf.

Lori R. Bramble
CAMBRIDGE, MARYLAND

We noticed this iridescent tree swallow on a rail fence while driving through Antietam National Battlefield in Maryland. Actually, we heard the swallow first, since he was making quite a noise. We weren't sure whether he was upset about something or just making a general announcement. I like to think that he was singing as loud as he could about the gorgeous summer day.

Anne Duvall
GREENCASTLE,
PENNSYLVANIA

A bluebird pair nested in a dead tree next to our pond, but one stormy night high winds broke a limb, sending both nest and young into the water. I discovered them the next day and I felt bad; the parents were flying around the tree in obvious distress.

As a participant in Minnesota's Bluebird Recovery Program, I had an extra bluebird box, which I put up near the original nest. It took a little bit but they finally settled in, and soon the pair was working hard to feed four new hatchlings.

Glenda Mueller ROCHESTER, MINNESOTA

Eastern bluebirds have a knack, as do so many other birds, for repurposing items to make their homes. These bluebirds have set up in my backyard owl decoy for several years, using wild turkey feathers for their nesting.

Cliff Beaver HUNTINGDON, PENNSYLVANIA

I'm amazed

by the striking red eyes and sleek black-and-white patterned bodies of loons, as well as how they ferry their chicks along on their backs for protection from predators. These sometimes elusive birds live on the lakes near my home, and when I photograph them I lie on the floor of the boat to shoot at their level.

Cari Povenz
GRANDVILLE, MICHIGAN

On a cloudy but bright day,

I caught this pair of American goldfinches taking advantage of the volunteer sunflowers in the garden. The male defended the flowers by chasing off any other birds attempting to enjoy the seeds. The pair would chatter between themselves while they cleaned out the sunflower heads. One day I observed their courtship ritual. The male flew to the side of the female, ruffled his head feathers and began feeding his mate. She fluttered her wings and ate the seeds he offered.

Jean Bullock
DU QUOIN, ILLINOIS

This is a Florida scrub-jay,

a threatened species in Florida due to habitat loss. I took the picture in Palatka, Florida, in a scrub ecosystem. I was with several friends snapping photos in the area, and the scrub-jay landed on one of the cameras and gave us a look. This picture shows how much personality these birds have—they are curious, friendly and full of sass!

Betty Walden
MERRITT ISLAND, FLORIDA

AT HOME
Florida scrub-jays have the distinction of being the only bird species that resides solely in Florida.

We visit southwest Florida every

year and love taking walks around our neighborhood. Our route goes by several empty lots where burrowing owls live. This year we were pleasantly surprised to find a pair with five precious owlets.

Mary Ann Clem
TERRE HAUTE, INDIANA

A first-year chestnut-sided warbler took about a dozen cautious passes above my backyard fountain and survived a couple of run-ins with the screened porch before it finally landed. I am so glad it did, because the pink begonias, white birch branch and the lime green in the warbler's feathers contrast beautifully, making this one of my favorite backyard photos.

Russ Ergen ST. CLOUD, MINNESOTA

There was a mallard that hatched 10 adorable ducklings in the raised planter alongside our pool. One morning, when they were ready to swim, they dropped one by one from the edge of the planter into the pool. We watched, charmed, until the mother tried showing them how to get out, and we saw that the water level was too low. Frantically, we pulled several hoses over, but the pool filled so slowly. Meanwhile, the female was growing exhausted.

My husband retrieved a long board and slid it into the water. While we watched from a window, the mother coaxed each duckling, one by one, up onto the ramp. They stayed on it for several hours, sunning and recovering from the ordeal.

After a day or so, they all left for a nearby lake, safely back in their natural habitat.

Carole Pinckney GREENVILLE, SOUTH CAROLINA

NOT PICKY EATERS
Eagles are opportunistic predators and scavengers, eating whatever is most accessible, from fish and small mammals to reptiles and other birds.

While vacationing in Washington state and exploring trails at La Push Beach, we came upon this juvenile bald eagle. I watched it pose for many pictures. Meanwhile, its parents perched nearby, keeping a watchful eye on their young. What an awesome sight!

Donna Scheumeister PORT ST. LUCIE, FLORIDA

I was super excited to find these orchard orioles, a male and a female, sharing the orange and jelly I put out! They kept visiting and eventually had a family that came to eat with them daily. They would always let me know when they were out of food!

Pam Garcia
MANSFIELD, LOUISIANA

The Carolina wren shown here is waiting in line for a chance at our feeder. This was also the premiere appearance of the honeysuckle vine we had planted the previous year, which wrapped itself around the tree.

Barry MacKichan
HILLSBOROUGH,
NORTH CAROLINA

Thrilled doesn't begin

to describe how I felt when a family of Gambel's quail ventured into my yard for lunch. After eating under my palo verde tree, Junior and his dad hopped up on my garden wall and posed perfectly for a quick photo.

After discovering that my property offers fine dining, the family of six became regular visitors. It's hard to believe how fast the young mature.

Nina Hansen
GREEN VALLEY, ARIZONA

ATTENTION GRABBING

Although both sexes of quail have a plume of black feathers atop their head, it's fuller in males.

When on vacation on

the Hawaiian island of Kauai, we were greeted each morning by these beautiful red-crested cardinals. When three of them landed on the deck railing, I used my telephoto lens to snap this picture. I call this photo "Take a Bow" because it seems as if they've just finished performing for us.

Susan Williams
VANCOUVER, WASHINGTON

Discovering this male dickcissel was the opposite of finding a
needle in a haystack. A cemetery behind a church in Peach Bottom, Pennsylvania,
had a dirt pile with some tall pokeweeds growing out of it. I never expected to find
the bird out in the open like this. Lucky me!

Mona Steinhauer LANCASTER, PENNSYLVANIA

While vacationing on Janes Island in Chesapeake Bay last August, I photographed this clapper rail near our camper. These birds are usually seen at low tide when the mudflats are exposed.

Christine Boltz HAMPSTEAD, MARYLAND

I became interested in birds one July and set out a hummingbird feeder. Near month's end, I was surprised to find not a hummingbird but this northern cardinal feeding his young. What a wonderful sight.

Keith Hopkin
SCARBOROUGH, ONTARIO

We have a cabin on Little Ossipee Lake in Maine. I was kayaking there one morning when I spotted a young loon and its parent. The adult went under and came up with a fish bigger than the offspring's head. I thought, "No way!" But the young loon flipped it up and gulped it right down!

Paul O'Malley
SAUGERTIES, NEW YORK

BELOW THE SURFACE
It's not often that you'll see an adult loon swallow a fish. Loons tend to catch and eat their prey underwater.

Grow Your Own Seed

Bring a landscape to life with money-saving plants that birds love.

By Tammi Hartung

DANNY BROWN

An American goldfinch plucks a seed from a sunflower head.

Yarrow plant varieties attract seed eaters such as pine siskins.

CHANCES ARE THAT BIRDS EAGERLY accept your open invitation to dine at your feeders. Make them more permanent guests by adding plants they love to eat.

In fact, the more bird-friendly plants you grow, the less time you spend filling feeders and buying seed. Plant a combination of seed-producing annuals and perennials to supply food year-round while saving time and money. Not all your favorite guests have the same palate, so diversity is key.

Serve Up the Perfect Plants

Lure more small songbirds to your garden with a selection of early-flowering perennials. Lavender, with its blue and purple flower stalks, bursts onto the garden scene in early summer. The purple spikes of anise hyssop bloom in early summer and continue into August, but some are very aggressive, so choose carefully. Yarrows, available in white and shades of yellow and pink, shine off and on throughout summer, too. To add a little color variation, consider columbines. Most columbines grow in full sun to part shade, but native varieties also work well in shady garden beds. All these perennials yield seed heads that are fantastic food sources for chickadees and juncos, especially after flowers have faded.

American goldfinches and other types of finches, along with pine siskins and indigo buntings, eat up the small seeds as well.

Summer's brightest blooms provide a buffet of food options for feathered friends. Purple coneflowers have beautiful purplish pink petals and burnt orange centers. After petals fade, the center cones have tasty seeds that nuthatches and pine siskins devour. Black-eyed Susans and sunflowers come alive in midsummer with cheerful yellow flowers for a colorful garden show well into early fall. Several seed eaters, including eastern and California towhees, forage these noninvasive plants.

The purple and pink blooms of buddleia bushes (choose noninvasive types) add color all summer and into fall. As flowers fade and seeds form, sparrows and finches feed on them. Joe Pye weed's mauve flowers complement showy fans of bright yellow goldenrod in late summer. Both dazzle into midautumn and attract indigo and lazuli buntings. And sedum works, too—many small songbirds feast on the dried flowers after the white, pink or yellow clusters fade.

Plan a Great Space

Growing plants for birds is certainly crucial, but it's just one part of the equation. Several other actions come together to create a well-rounded

Joe Pye weed

Most Wanted Birds
Look for these seed eaters flitting from plant to plant.

- Chickadees
- Dark-eyed juncos
- Goldfinches
- Grosbeaks
- House finches
- Northern cardinals
- Nuthatches
- Pine siskins
- Purple finches

Add water to make your yard more appealing to birds.

The Secret Is in the Sunflowers

Plant several of these varieties to get more birds for your buck.

Autumn Beauty: multiple flowers in yellow, burgundy and gold

Fat Mama: traditional with fat flower heads

Lyng's California Greystripe: large yellow flowers that give way to gray and white striped seeds

Maximilian: multibranched with lots of 3-inch yellow blooms

Mexican (Tithonia): loads of orange flowers that attract pollinators

Moulin Rouge: deep burgundy petals with a rich black center

Ring of Fire: yellow petals with a dark red ring around the center

Strawberry Blonde: lemony tips and rose-pink petals with a dark center

Taiyo: a Japanese heirloom with large chocolate brown centers and short yellow petals

Teddy Bear: double yellow flowers on dwarf plants

and thriving environment that attracts multiple bird species.

Be cautious about using chemicals. Direct-contact or broadcast applications are harmful if birds eat seeds treated with insecticides or synthetic pesticides. Because chemicals leave residue inside plant parts for up to 18 months, it's best to keep natural spaces free of any pesticides, fungicides and herbicides.

Next, set up a good water source to help birds wash down a meal. Birds need only about an inch of water, but if your birdbath is somewhat deep, add a good-sized rock in the center as a solid perching spot.

When all the flowers have flourished for the season, keep your garden intact. The less tidying you do, the better. Leave dried flower heads in place for foraging winter birds. Cut back and clean up last year's stalks in late winter and early spring when you're ready to prep for the new season.

Once you attract seed eaters to your space, you won't want them to leave. Small songbirds provide hours of entertainment and delight as they forage and find food. But more important, the habitat you create gives your favorite fliers a much-needed healthy haven to return to.

LEFT: FRANCIS & JANICE BERGQUIST; RIGHT: BILL LEAMAN

Sunflowers
lure songbirds,
such as this
song sparrow to
your backyard.

Making It Out of the Nest

Peer through your binoculars and see if you can spot the differences between young and adult birds.

By Ken Keffer

SUMMER IS THE SEASON WHEN juvenile birds develop their wing feathers (a process called fledging) and begin to explore the world beyond the nest. It's a fantastic time to bird-watch, but a few of these youngsters are tricky to recognize, thanks to camouflage coloring. If you know what to look for, you can be ready when one flies across your path.

American Robin

Baby birds often don't resemble their parents, and young robins are a classic example. Like deer fawns, they have bold spots during their first summer, with buff speckling along their backs and breasts. Watch as they scamper across the lawn, mimicking the red-breasted adults as they hunt for worms and other invertebrates.

Notice the prominent spots on the juvenile robin's back.

Male American redstarts have bold black-and-orange coloring. But 1-year-old males (bottom) are subtly colored, like females.

American Redstart

For this species of warbler, the resemblance between the young birds and the adult females continues beyond the first fall. During the second summer, a few black feathers show up on the males to set them apart from females, but it isn't until later in the season that the male redstarts molt into full black-and-orange plumage.

Young Bird Basics

These telltale signs separate the kids from the grown-ups.

- Juveniles often have a soft, fluffy look, even beyond the down feather nestling stage.

- A fleshy gape—the area where the upper and lower bills connect—is a hint you're looking at an immature bird.

- After they leave the nest, they still exhibit food-begging behavior. However, in some species, this is also a courtship ritual of adults.

- Like toddlers learning to walk, growing birds can be awkward in flight. Landings are especially tricky.

- Young birds may seem helpless, but they're tougher than you think. It's best to give them their space and let them be.

A male northern cardinal feeds his offspring. Below, a fledgling cardinal (right) typically appears disheveled, but even more so when enjoying a bath with its mom.

TOP: MARIE READ; BOTTOM: STEVE AND DAVE MASLOWSKI

Northern Cardinal

Adolescent northern cardinals always look as if they have bed head because of a thin wispy crest of feathers. They also have nearly black beaks, which lighten up as the summer progresses and, come autumn, have the characteristic red-orange bill of the species. By then, a few scarlet body feathers are observable on young males, too, but until that time both sexes appear similar to adult females.

White-crowned Sparrow

Sometimes sparrows are affectionately called "little brown jobs." Their immature plumage makes them even more nondescript, but one species that stands out during immaturity is the white-crowned sparrow. The bold nutmeg brown stripes on top of its head are a good field mark. These birds typically turn black and white the following spring, when the bird is almost a year old.

Before young white-crowneds get their distinct plumage, they sport brown and tan stripes.

CHRISTINE HAINES

Identify growing downies by their red caps. Adult males (left) have smaller red patches.

Downy Woodpecker

You've probably seen black-and-white downy woodpeckers flying through your backyard, but during the summer months you may have noticed some with extensive red on their foreheads and crowns. These are young downies, and both sexes wear this red initially, although it's much more widespread on males. (Adult female downy woodpeckers have no scarlet markings at all.) Use binoculars to observe the dark browns in the wings of these birds compared with the black feathers of the adults.

Brown-headed Cowbird

Occasionally, something about a bird family doesn't seem quite right. Maybe a tiny yellow warbler is feeding a much larger bird, or a wood thrush has a tagalong with a thicker bill and streaky markings. Brown-headed cowbirds are nest parasites, which means females lay eggs in the nests of other species. They hatch quickly, and the host parents raise the larger, grayish-brown cowbird young. Many species involuntarily host cowbird eggs, so these young birds are always mismatched with the adults that are raising them.

A song sparrow feeds a much larger immature cowbird.

FROM TOP: MARIE READ; CAROL L. EDWARDS

This adult heron has deep color in its eyes and an ebony crown, unlike the colors of the juvenile heron (bottom).

Black-crowned Night-Heron

Once it's all grown up, this wetland species is quite stately, with thick black bills, ebony crowns and backs, and gray wings and bodies that fade into lighter-hued bellies. Young birds, however, appear more like bitterns than night-herons because of their broad brown streaks. Their bills have lots of yellow that slowly turns black, and their eyes start off yellow-orange but gain richer color over time, eventually turning nearly red.

Red-headed Woodpecker

Many woodpeckers have red coloring on their heads, but one of the few with an entirely red head is, you guessed it, the red-headed woodpecker. Confusingly, the juvenile has a brown head and heavy brown markings that break up the rest of its pattern. Watch for broad flashes of white across the wings, lower back and rump, contrasting with the darker upper back, wingtips and tail. By fall, some red feathers may appear on the head, but many brown feathers may be retained in the next year.

It may take almost a full year for an immature red-headed woodpecker to grow all of its red feathers.

MARIE READ

CHAPTER 3

Fall

At the first hint of autumn, birds are active and focused, either starting their migration or planning for their stay through the winter months.

During the first wave of fall migration, I was in my backyard taking pictures of birds when this female American redstart appeared at my water fountain. She was very excited to see water and kept hopping back and forth, fanning her tail feathers. After several minutes, she finally took the plunge and jumped in, spending a few minutes splashing in the water.

Linda Petersen
TERRIL, IOWA

I heard about red-breasted nuthatch sightings in the area, and I was thrilled to find the bird on my new sunflower feeder. I'm not sure if it was attracted to the new feeder specifically, but I'm glad it came!

Nancy Tully
EAST STROUDSBURG,
PENNSYLVANIA

The fall leaf colors created a wonderful reflection on the serene water at Sterne Park in Littleton, Colorado. I captured the scene, along with a male wood duck, with my Canon 5D Mark IV.

Robert Magee DENVER, COLORADO

Early one morning while out birding, I saw a pair of northern cardinals. This female and her mate were both eating berries from a tree. I really like how the female stood out against the scenery of the woods.

Andy Raupp MONTELLO, WISCONSIN

When I first saw this bird, I had no idea what it was. It wasn't one that we commonly see in our backyard in the foothills of North Carolina. I was surprised and delighted to learn that it was a yellow-billed cuckoo. I haven't seen it since, although I have heard its call coming from the woods surrounding our home a couple of times.

Sandra Adams
BOONVILLE,
NORTH CAROLINA

IN THE TREES
Yellow-billed cuckoos are seen in most of the eastern United States, but the fliers are often overlooked in their dense forest homes.

I feed blue jays peanuts every morning and afternoon in my backyard. If they run out of peanuts on the patio, they start calling loudly. But as long as they have their treats, they don't seem to bully the birds at my feeders. This blue jay posed for me after carefully selecting a peanut. I took the photo in fall, when the jays are typically busy stashing peanuts for winter.

Anne Duvall
GREENCASTLE,
PENNSYLVANIA

The fall colors reflecting in the water at Stanley Park in Westfield, Massachusetts, make it look as if this mute swan is swimming in a golden pond. I took the photo with a Nikon D750 and Nikon 70-300 mm lens.

Marc St. Onge
RUSSELL, MASSACHUSETTS

When they return in the fall, warblers seem to favor native plants as sources for insects and caterpillars. I spotted a Nashville warbler moving among the goldenrods, so I knelt down a bit to conceal myself. I waited for the bird to get close enough that I could snap this pretty photo.

Travis Bonovsky
BROOKLYN CENTER, MINNESOTA

I was on an autumn hike in search of birds to photograph. It was very quiet, so I headed back to my car. That's when I noticed some activity coming from a cluster of rose bushes. To my delight, it was a flock of cedar waxwings dining on small red rose hips. In a matter of minutes, they raided all of the bushes and quickly moved on.

Sharon Cuartero DANBURY, CONNECTICUT

I stocked my feeders with sunflower seeds in fall after hearing about an evening grosbeak irruption. Sure enough, a single male grosbeak showed up and stayed for two days. He was briefly joined by three females, too.

Nancy Tully EAST STROUDSBURG, PENNSYLVANIA

The California scrub-jays were vocal on the morning that I took this photo. A jay with an acorn in its beak settled briefly on an outer branch of a coast live oak. I had only a few moments to capture it flying away to its next spot. The timing of this photo is perfect as it shows the bird leaping off with one wing spread while the other was unfurling.

Sandeep Dhar
SAN DIEGO, CALIFORNIA

When nuthatches are everywhere, you know cooler weather isn't far behind. I love watching the white-breasted nuthatches that become more active with the changing seasons.

Laura Frazier
KEARNEYSVILLE,
WEST VIRGINIA

My husband

and I enjoy watching the birds and wildlife in our rural backyard. It's not unusual to see pheasants, deer or even wild turkeys wandering through. One time, we had the pleasure of watching two juvenile bald eagles at our birdbath, sometimes staying as long as three hours. This is the first time we've had anything this size using it.

Irene Swartzer
WATERTOWN, MINNESOTA

Robins are regular visitors

throughout the year. They take over my crabapple tree when the fruit ripens in November and December, fiercely defending the tree's fruit. It's amazing to watch and to capture all the activity.

Sharon Sauriol
WASHINGTON, MICHIGAN

TASTY BERRIES

Crabapples are the ultimate wildlife-friendly trees, providing shelter and plenty of fruit.

This was the first time I saw a green-winged teal, although many ducks are found in my area. The reflection in the water really makes the photo special—it helps the wing's iridescence pop. I was super thankful to get this shot.

Katie Myer SANDUSKY, OHIO

I always enjoy my backyard birds. One of my favorite things is setting up scenes for them to visit. I just put out food, and they will come. This Carolina chickadee stopped by to grab a snack. I love capturing them from behind the camera.

Jacqueline Hodsdon FOREST, VIRGINIA

Fall in Ohio

is such a lovely time of year. The vegetation begins to change, birds are migrating south and the heat has subsided. When I reflect on the season, I think of this magnolia warbler photo that I took by Chippewa Lake in Ohio.

Debbie Parker
MEDINA, OHIO

It was such an honor to watch this barred owl in a tree behind my fence all afternoon. The bird had a nice, lazy Sunday while posing for my camera. It didn't seem to mind me at all, as you can see by its big yawn between preening times.

Jennifer Rush
GRESHAM, OREGON

I dried a number of sunflowers to use as a food source in my yard for birds, such as this black-capped chickadee. My feathered guests really enjoy these organic feeders.

Monica Brill MOUNT MORRIS, NEW YORK

A tufted titmouse

enjoyed some corn at a feeding station in Dorothy Carnes County Park near Fort Atkinson, Wisconsin. I don't have titmice at my own feeders very often, so I was thrilled to spend some time with this little cutie.

Barbara Houlihan
MADISON, WISCONSIN

I photographed

this pair of wood ducks on a pond near our home. I've provided two wood duck nest boxes that have been used for the past decade. I took the photo with my Canon EOS 70D.

Edward Price
ROCKLIN, CALIFORNIA

BRILLIANT IN BLUE
Wood ducks, both male and female, have blue and white wing plumage.

PURPLE TREATS
American beautyberries are easily recognized in autumn. Bright purple berries that birds adore appear in clusters, and the leaves start to turn yellow and orange.

A flock of American robins landed on a large beautyberry bush in my backyard one November. I enjoy this image, which I used a Nikon telephoto lens to capture, because of the colors and pose of the bird.

Darryl Neill DECATUR, GEORGIA

HIDE & SEEK
Woodcocks are perfectly camouflaged on forest floors, the ideal place for them to probe the ground for earthworms.

My husband, Troy, and I saw the most amazing little bird while on an early trip to a nearby lake. At first I thought it was a dove, all fluffed up and trying to keep warm. On closer inspection, this bird's feathers were more bronze and almost glittery, and its bill was as long as its body. I photographed it, and got out the bird book when I was back at home. It turns out our mystery bird is an American woodcock!

Melody Hill SALEM, INDIANA

Blue jays
showed up in my
backyard regularly
after I filled this
pumpkin with seeds.

Victoria Schwinabart
SWANTON, MARYLAND

**On a cold,
rainy October
afternoon,**
our feeders were
overwhelmed by a flock
of pine siskins. We had
seen one of these birds
in the yard a couple of
times, but this was wild!
The competition for food
was fierce among the
many birds; they kept
snipping their beaks at
one another, protecting
their snack supply. I got
a number of entertaining
action shots.

Ginger Culp
GURNEE, ILLINOIS

I was enjoying a sunny, refreshing fall morning when a family of eastern bluebirds showed up. After they romped around the treetops for a while, I went inside. When I came back out, they were checking out this birdhouse. I think they wanted to put down a deposit for next year!

Kimberly Miskiewicz
RALEIGH,
NORTH CAROLINA

I captured this photo of a male spotted towhee while he was perched on some sagebrush along the public walking trail by the Encinitas Ranch Golf Course.

Bob Turner
ENCINITAS, CALIFORNIA

The Canada geese on Shelter Island in New York are absolutely stunning. I like to go when the lighting is ideal and reflections are at their best. I found this goose in the perfect spot—it was as if he were posing for a portrait.

Adam Bundy SHELTER ISLAND, NEW YORK

A beautiful great blue heron stops by every day, and I caught this image while it was preening along the banks of the lake in my backyard. I adore the plumage of these elegant water birds.

Kathryn Herndon FLORAL CITY, FLORIDA

A black-capped chickadee was getting ready to dive onto my feeder. Although they are common around my neighborhood, they're still among my favorites.

Raven Ouellette
SUDBURY, ONTARIO

The first time

I encountered a northern flicker, I was walking home from a friend's house in early fall. Its call, an interesting bellow that echoed through the neighborhood from the top of a large oak tree, caught my attention first. I captured a few photos of the flicker, but later sadly realized I had forgotten to put a memory card in my camera. Luckily, this friendly flicker decided to absolve me of my novice mistake a few months later.

Shane Etter
MERRICK, NEW YORK

The Carolina wren can be found in most of the Eastern United States. Even though I see them often in my home state of North Carolina, I still delight at their beautiful cinnamon plumage.

Kimberly Miskiewicz
RALEIGH,
NORTH CAROLINA

WOODLAND SINGERS

Carolina wrens have a repetitive three-note song that sounds like *teakettle* or *Germany*, depending on which birder you ask.

This is one of my favorite photos, and it was an accident! One day I saw three toms strutting their stuff through my back window and took photos of the boys showing off. Later, while I was uploading my shots, I noticed that the heads of these two form a heart.

Kristine Cooley
WAYZATA, MINNESOTA

I have tried for years to photograph a scissor-tailed flycatcher, so when I stopped in a parking lot to take a phone call and spotted this one, I grabbed my telephoto lens with excitement. The bird was about 20 feet away in a tree, and as I snapped away, I inched my car toward it, expecting it to fly away any second.

As I pulled next to the trees, I just kept my finger on the shutter. The flycatcher kept moving around, at one point jumping to the ground and flying right back up with a grasshopper. When I got home and downloaded the pictures, I saw I had captured the bird throwing the grasshopper in the air, turning it around and catching it. I can't describe how thrilled I was to have these awesome photos. I took over 500 pictures and had six super shots.

Linda Greco ROWLETT, TEXAS

During fall migration, sandhill cranes gather near Crex Meadows Wildlife Area in Wisconsin. Dozens of birds make their way to local farm fields to feed on leftover corn and grain from the harvest.

Jeff Sanders LA CROSSE, WISCONSIN

BROAD PALATE

Sandhill cranes will eat both plants and small animals. Look for them picking at agricultural fields during migration.

Friends told us that they'd spotted a great horned owl nest high in a neighbor's pine tree, and when my wife and I went to look, we were delighted to discover an unobstructed view from a bridge. We returned repeatedly until the two owlets were large enough to stand tall on the nest. With a parent in attendance, they allowed us to take this telephoto family portrait.

Jack Hailman JUPITER, FLORIDA

The most common bird

at our feeders is the house finch. I most often see them with a red head, but occasionally one with a yellow or orange head will appear. I took this photo at Red Rocks Park near Denver, Colorado. This male shows off his red rump ever so nicely.

Carl Muehlemeyer
BROOMFIELD, COLORADO

As I walked around my house,

a blue jay stopped me in my tracks. I had left my sunflowers standing for the birds to eat, but I didn't expect to see this. The jay quickly flew off even though I backed up slowly so I wouldn't startle it. After grabbing my camera, I went back outside and heard the blue jay again, from a distance. I knew it was coming back so I waited at the corner of the house until, sure enough, it returned for the sunflower seeds.

Steve Henderson
COLEMAN, MICHIGAN

At first, I laid out peanuts to try to photograph some squirrels, but then I decided to put some peanuts in the birdbath, too. I set up my bird blind, and that's when this grackle landed to snatch up a peanut. Before it could fly off, I captured what looks like an angry expression. I feel as though the grackle is saying, "Don't even think about taking this peanut from me!"

Jimmy Hartnett
CHARLESTON,
SOUTH CAROLINA

I took this photo of Mr. and Mrs. Painted Bunting near Surf City, North Carolina. They were having dinner before heading south for the winter. At the time, I couldn't help wishing I was going along with them.

George Johnson
RALEIGH,
NORTH CAROLINA

I came across a solitary sandpiper at a nearby pond. And although solitary is part of its name, I consistently saw this bird hanging out with a group of mallards. One visit to the pond coincided with the peak of fall colors, so I was lucky to see the sandpiper position itself among some vibrant hues and stretch its wings.

Michael Rossacci ARLINGTON, MASSACHUSETTS

NO NUTS ABOUT IT
If you can't attract titmice with peanuts during winter, try their favorite: sunflower seeds.

Our tufted titmouse has a real taste for peanuts. It will take a nut to our maple tree, lodge it in the bark and peck it into small enough pieces to eat.

John Chaille MUNCIE, INDIANA

Seeing this female rose-breasted grosbeak was a surprise! We were lucky to have the male and female visit in spring, but this was the first time I saw a grosbeak in fall. Her mate is more striking in appearance, but she is a beauty!

Jennifer Hardison
ATHENS, TENNESSEE

One day, while standing in the front yard, I noticed northern flickers enjoying the red berries on our dogwood tree. The autumn colors of the tree and the flicker's colors really make this shot. The birds came back several times until all the berries were gone.

Gary LeValley
WALLA WALLA, WASHINGTON

I spied this male wood duck in a marsh near Portage, Wisconsin, and was fortunate to get a good photograph. What I enjoy most are the brilliant colors and how the blurred background shows the duck's movement as he leaves the water.

Trevor Ruff
BARABOO, WISCONSIN

HEAD'S UP!
Wood ducks hold their heads up high while in flight, at times bobbing them.

A Carolina chickadee nabbed a seed from our feeder and flew to a nearby branch to eat it. Several other birds circled around trying to take it away, but the chickadee fought them off, then set to work opening it. After all that work, the chickadee suddenly dropped it. The poor bird looked at the seed on the ground and then at me, back and forth, before it flew away. The photo is funny, but I did feel bad for that little chickadee.

Houston Pittman
PICAYUNE, MISSISSIPPI

One year the Midwest had quite a finch irruption, with wide reports of red crossbills, white-winged crossbills and pine siskins at backyard feeders.

Pine siskins became daily visitors to my feeder in early November, often in flocks of two dozen or more. When they couldn't find room at the feeder, they would head to the garden to pick any remaining seeds from spent flower heads. Here's one snacking away in my Little Chief crape myrtle bush.

Mary Nemecek KANSAS CITY, MISSOURI

This downy woodpecker must have grown tired of carrying seeds into trees to crack them and eat the kernels. It dug a hole in a dead limb next to the feeder, where, with little effort, it could grab a seed, trap it and hammer out the innards. Smart little bird.

Norman Cline MOUNT CARMEL, ILLINOIS

I captured this moment of pure delight for a western scrub-jay as it splashed in water. I love the way it enjoyed its bath by flinging water around.

Patricia Marshall
RIO RANCHO,
NEW MEXICO

Some people find blue jays aggressive and unappreciative at feeders, but to me they're beautiful and majestic. For several years, they've been rare in our neighborhood, so when this one came along one fall to snack on sunflower seeds, I felt fortunate to get its photo. I saw it just twice more, and both times it behaved nicely at my feeders, happy to share with the chickadees, titmice, goldfinches and cardinals. Blue jays are welcome in my yard anytime!

Robin Seeber
WEST ALEXANDER,
PENNSYLVANIA

A JAY'S JOYS
What do blue jays hope to see at your feeders? Sunflower seeds, suet and plenty of peanuts!

I saw this male yellow-bellied sapsucker near our home for several days before I noticed this distinctive pattern on the holly tree and realized he must be the culprit. It took a long wait with my camera to capture his face and the gorgeous markings down his back. What an awesome bird!

Barbara Carter
LAURENS, SOUTH CAROLINA

SUCKERS FOR SAP
These shallow holes on trees require continued attention by the birds to keep the sap flowing, so if you see them, you may see sapsuckers returning to them.

I **took** this photo of a juvenile little blue heron a few years ago. The bird seemed to pose perfectly for a picture, and I loved the composition. The contrast of the white bird against the green tree and Spanish moss was really eye-catching.

Lois Bange
MCDONALD, TENNESSEE

One fall, I heard there would be a chance of seeing evening grosbeaks in our area. The previous time I saw one was years earlier. Sure enough, these gorgeous creatures stopped by my feeder for several visits.

Nancy Tully
EAST STROUDSBURG,
PENNSYLVANIA

UNUSUAL SONGS

Instead of singing complex tunes to attract mates, evening grosbeaks sound a few chirps and notes.

People are always surprised when I say how much I love European starlings, but how can anyone not love them? Their feathers have a plethora of colors, they eat annoying bugs and they're smart enough to mimic other songbirds. This one finally became brave enough to come close to the feeder while I was there with my camera.

Robin Seeber WEST ALEXANDER, PENNSYLVANIA

This burrowing owl was perched on a fence post on a busy road when I first saw it. I went back for two more days, watching it and snapping photos. I really like this photo because you can see it thoughtfully observing the bug above its head.

Brenda Werbelow WINDSOR, COLORADO

At a nearby lake where I like to photograph birds, white pelicans make their appearance in spring and then leave just before winter. One cold autumn morning, the pelicans were just becoming active. This one was circling me before it decided to land, so I waited for just the right moment. What I like about this image is how it captures the movement of the pelican's wings in the early-morning fog.

Dennis Adams
BURNEY, CALIFORNIA

I was really happy to see this beautiful male northern flicker at my suet feeder. He was there for only a very short time before a starling came and chased him away.

Fran Marple
YORK, PENNSYLVANIA

After hearing

northern bobwhites for quite some time but barely catching a glimpse of any, I finally came face to face with one for the first time. One day, wood ducks flew overhead and landed near a marshy area of our property. While I walked through the bog to look for the ducks, I glanced over and saw this bobwhite sitting on a stump. It hopped down, stayed around the brush under the tree for a bit, then jumped up onto a branch, where it stayed for quite some time. It was very close, and I was so excited that it was hard to stay calm. I finally got a good bobwhite picture.

Georgia Wilson
GENEVA, FLORIDA

While walking

in Wisconsin's Whitefish Dunes State Park one fall, I came upon a pair of pileated woodpeckers. Strangely enough, they were not on the trunk of the tree, but hanging from branches and eating black cherries. I had never seen this before and was happy to watch for a good 20 minutes, as well as take pictures.

Carrol Fibich
BROOKFIELD, WISCONSIN

It amazes me that the smallest birds seem to be the most curious. Like hummingbirds and chickadees, this pygmy nuthatch had a very friendly disposition! It contentedly foraged around the branches just a few feet away and kindly sat still for photos. I was thrilled to discover the existence of this adorable little bird and look forward to seeing it again for future photo sessions.

Joan Zeiber MISSOULA, MONTANA

SNOW BIRDS
To stay warm during winter nights, redpolls will sometimes tunnel into the snow.

After other birds have gone south, redpolls descend on us from the far north. Small but brave, these hardy finches give us joy in an otherwise drab and dreary season.

Laurenz Baars PEACE RIVER, ALBERTA

The bright red of this cardinal sitting on the top of a mimosa tree in the morning sun caught my eye. This cardinal is one half of a pair that lives in my backyard.

Jack Dunaway
WAXAHACHIE, TEXAS

I enjoy quite a variety of woodpeckers at my feeding station, and as you can see, sometimes all at the same time! Here, a red-bellied seems to be on the lookout while a red-headed and a hairy woodpecker sample the suet.

Mary Roberts-Young
SPARTA, TENNESSEE

SUET WILL DO IT!

In general, a woodpeckers' favorite feeder foods are suet, suet and suet! Offer it in cooler weather, when insects become scarce to find.

Molting Masters of Disguise

Now you see them, now you don't! Discover why birds change color in the fall and how to identify them.

By Kenn and Kimberly Kaufman

In the fall, male American goldfinches lose their brilliant yellow feathers (left), and new brown ones grow in instead. This process is called molting.

Male scarlet tanagers change from red and black to dull yellow (far right) in late summer.

A S SUMMER SLIPS INTO FALL AND the weather cools down, swimsuits and shorts are swapped for sweaters and scarves. Birds also change their wardrobes with the seasons. Many species look the same 365 days of the year, but some look so different in fall that they are challenging to identify.

Disappearing Act

Take the American goldfinch, for example. All summer, glowing yellow male American goldfinches nibble at your feeder, and then one fall day there's not a bright lemon-colored songbird to be found. In fact, the goldfinches are still around and coming to feeders. They just look different—drab and dull. The color changes of the female American goldfinch are subtle, but the male is all drama. He transitions from blazing yellow to a much duller yellow-brown, making him look more like the female.

His feathers aren't actually changing color. Instead, the bird gradually replaces all the feathers in a process called molting. Over the span of a few weeks, old feathers slowly drop out and new ones grow in. If you spot the male goldfinch in the middle of molting, he'll have patches of yellow and brown. But once he's decked out in his autumn garb, you'd never guess he was once bright yellow.

Presto Change-O

Molting isn't just unique to goldfinches. As a rule, any healthy wild songbird replaces its feathers at least once a year. Late summer to fall is the most common time for this to happen, but in many cases it's not too noticeable. A male cardinal, for example, replaces old red feathers with new red feathers, so he looks freshened up but otherwise unchanged. It's another story, of course, when birds molt into a completely different plumage in fall.

One bird that changes in a big way is the male scarlet tanager, which is scarlet for only half the year. In late summer, this species replaces all its

feathers before migrating to South America in fall. The male plumage changes from brilliant red to dull yellowish-green, like the female's. The same thing happens to the bobolink of meadows and hayfields. The male bobolink's breeding plumage of black, yellow and white is replaced by a yellowish brown sparrowlike pattern before he flies off to South America in fall. The male indigo bunting goes from an intense deep blue in spring and summer to mostly brown.

Fledgling Feats

In late summer a new challenge comes as young birds leave the nest, looking very different from their parents. Baby chipping sparrows are covered with dark streaks, while their parents have smooth gray chests and reddish caps. Fledgling robins and bluebirds are covered with spots at first but eventually lose them as they grow up. The majority of small birds, however, molt their body and head feathers soon after they become independent, quickly replacing their

Young cedar waxwings (left) and adults sport yellow bands on their tails. Use that clue to identify tricky juveniles in fall.

juvenile plumage. Within a month, they look recognizably similar to adults.

Once fall arrives, some young birds look very different. Cedar waxwings usually nest late in summer, so you might see streaky brown juveniles as late as November. Young red-headed woodpeckers have brown heads until late fall and occasionally through winter. While adult white-crowned sparrows are smooth gray and brown with sharp black and white head stripes, their young have brown and tan stripes on their heads through their first fall and winter.

Crack the Code

The good news is that as tough as it can be to identify adults that change color or youngsters that look different from their parents, it's not impossible. For starters, when you see an odd bird in fall, look beyond its colors and focus on its shape, size and actions. Even without bright hues, a male scarlet tanager is still a medium-size songbird with a thick bill that moves quietly through the foliage in tall trees. Although a young cedar waxwing has stripes on its chest, it's still

a crested bird that sits upright, eats berries and flies out to catch insects in midair. It's also likely to be in a flock with other waxwings.

Another tried-and-true tip is to look closely at the wings and tail. On most birds, these don't change as much as the head and body do. That male scarlet tanager may be mostly greenish yellow in autumn, but he still has black wings. The young cedar waxwing has a yellow band at the tip of its tail, just like the adults.

A good way to practice fall bird ID skills is to look at those American goldfinches again. The males lose their bold color, but they're still tiny birds with thick, seed-crunching beaks. They're still active and sociable, moving around in flocks, with a bouncy flight and short musical calls. They still have black wings with white or buff wing bars, and white spots on black tails. The bright gold color may be gone, but that goldfinch personality is always present.

Soon it'll be spring again. Watch your feeders and you may witness a magical transformation as the goldfinches go from patchy brown and yellow on the way to a sparkling summer wardrobe.

Eastern bluebirds quickly lose their spotty juvenile feathers as they grow up.

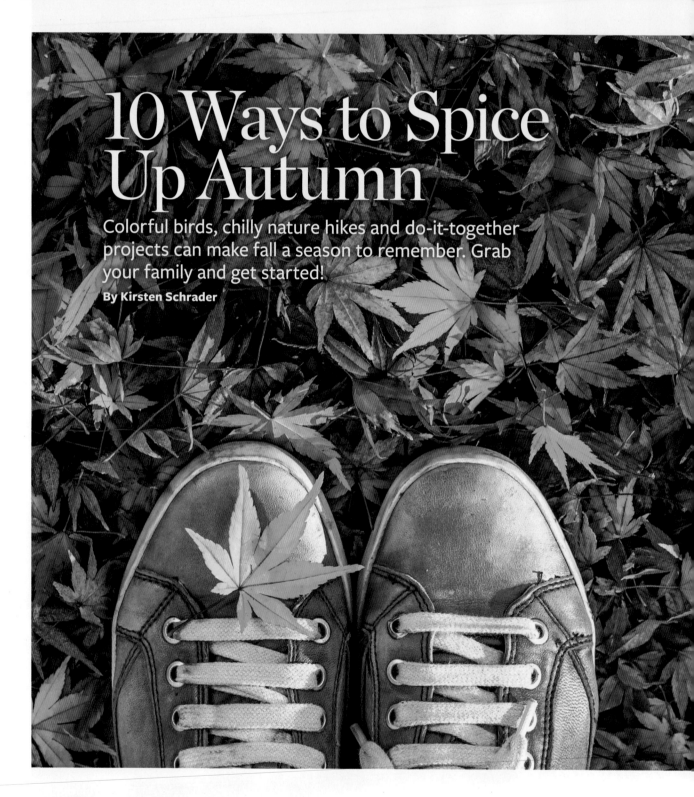

10 Ways to Spice Up Autumn

Colorful birds, chilly nature hikes and do-it-together projects can make fall a season to remember. Grab your family and get started!

By Kirsten Schrader

1 Ready, Set, LEAP!

Rake your leaves into a huge pile. Gather up the youngsters in your life and show 'em how it's done—jump in, challenge them to a leaf fight or noisily tromp through the crisp and crunchy heap. You'll feel like a kid again.

2 Attract More Jays

Brilliantly colored blue jays are a welcome backyard sight among the brassy colors of fall. The key to luring these flashy and boisterous fliers is peanuts, one of their favorite foods! Place the treats (either in or out of the shell) on a tray feeder or in a feeder made specifically for peanuts.

LEFT: JAVARMAN/SHUTTERSTOCK; RIGHT: STEVE AND DAVE MASLOWSKI

3

Light Up Your Backyard

No outdoor fireplace? No problem! Put several inexpensive pillar candles under a cloche or cover and set your patio aglow at dusk. Amp up the fall vibe by adding some gourds or small pumpkins. Settle in with a steaming cup of hot apple cider and enjoy the ambiance.

Many fall fliers, such as this downy woodpecker, love suet.

4

Serve Suet

Buy ready-made cakes and slide them right into a suet feeder. Or try this DIY version: Melt 1 cup shortening and 2 cups chunky peanut butter over low heat. Mix in 5 cups cornmeal. Pour into muffin tin. Sprinkle each cake with your choice of nuts, birdseed or dried berries. Cool in the refrigerator.

TOP LEFT: GAP PHOTOS/FRIEDRICH STRAUSS; BOTTOM LEFT: LAURIE STUCHLIK; RIGHT: GAP PHOTOS/VISIONS

5 Add Festive Flair

While you're visiting the pumpkin farm or apple orchard, grab a few extra items and use them to add a harvestlike touch to a display in your backyard or on your front porch. Let the kids choose their favorite spotted or striped gourd.

6 Bring the Outdoors In

Make a wreath from your garden's bounty or farmers market finds: crabapples or berry branches, sunflower or other seed heads, hydrangea blooms, ornamental cucumbers, and twigs or branches.

7

Create Photo Ops

Make a mini photo studio in your backyard with pumpkins, gourds or leaves. Sprinkle some birdseed throughout your scene and snap pics when the birds arrive.

8

Hit the Trails

Put on some comfy shoes and grab a light jacket for a hike. Whether you make it a quick stroll or a daylong adventure complete with a picnic, remember to pack your binoculars and a field guide!

9 Watch for Migrants

Fall bird migration begins as early as June but lasts through December. Strong cold fronts with low-pressure centers boost migration and cause fallouts. That's when large groups, sometimes in the thousands, converge in one spot. Always keep your binoculars handy.

10   Warm Up with a Bonfire

Invite your neighbors, family and friends over for an evening bonfire. Set out a few snacks, a stash of spare blankets and marshmallows for s'mores. While you're sitting by a crackling fire, listen for your neighborhood owls and watch for bats flying overhead or moths looking for light.

CHAPTER 4

Winter

Not all birds turn tail and fly when the cold comes rolling in—many stick around. Enjoy welcome sightings of these species and keep an eye out for those just passing through.

While shoveling snow from our walkways and patio, my husband and I noticed this spotted towhee jetting back and forth between the pine trees, fruit trees and our bird feeders. He would wait for the starlings to scratch the feed into the snow and then swoop in for a morsel or two. We don't see the towhees often, so it was nice to spot this male on such a snowy, cold day.

Christine Robinson CHINO VALLEY, ARIZONA

Northern Alabama got an unusual amount of snow one year, and this male northern cardinal was trying to stay warm in the cold. I've always wanted a shot of a cardinal in the snow! The snow lasted three days with temperatures in the upper 20s to mid-30s. It was a great opportunity to get out, since most businesses are not open when it snows here.

Jack Peterson
HUNTSVILLE, ALABAMA

Every winter I look forward to the arrival of the common redpolls. Last year they appeared later than usual, but it's always such a nice surprise when they show up.

Lilly Hiebert
DRUMHELLER, ALBERTA

In January, this partial leucistic female cardinal began visiting my feeder just after the start of the New Year. She is so beautiful, and I am so lucky!

Kathy Freeborn
WEST GROVE, PENNSYLVANIA

During some historic cold weather in Texas one February, a greater roadrunner was puffed up in my crepe myrtle to keep warm. I took this shot from my kitchen window on a blustery day.

Kathie Wiederspan
INGRAM, TEXAS

SHORT FLIGHTS

True to its name, a greater roadrunner is more skilled on land than in the air. It mainly flies from perch to perch or to the ground.

LITTLE THIEF
White-breasted nuthatches can be crafty during winter, sometimes stealing from other birds' food caches.

Hello from my backyard nuthatch! I was very lucky to get a cool shot of this cutie. My husband recently put our feeders back up; they'd been down all summer because of black bears. I love trying to get unusual shots of birds and other wildlife.

Sheryl Fleming HOFFMEISTER, NEW YORK

Flocks of goldfinches visited my yard and feeders last winter. They would sometimes all perch together in the sumacs nearby. I was super excited to capture this photo of a male goldfinch taking flight from one of the sumac branches.

Andy Raupp MONTELLO, WISCONSIN

I spotted this

American robin when I was walking at Riverside Park in Guelph, Ontario, on a gorgeous winter morning. It was one of several birds snacking on the berries.

Brenda Doherty
ARISS, ONTARIO

On a wintry day, some Anna's hummingbirds were resting in a Japanese maple tree in my backyard. It made my day to watch them. I took this photo with a Canon Powershot SX710 HS camera.

Patti Rust
LACEY, WASHINGTON

I photographed this male house finch on my deck during a blizzard. I sent a copy of the image to my Aunt Jo and Uncle Stan, who became permanent snowbirds when they retired from Ohio and relocated to Orlando, Florida. I accompanied the fascinating photograph with the caption, "This is what we Northerners call snowbirds."

Mike Droppleman
NORTON, OHIO

A male eastern towhee was hanging out near my backyard feeder. I have been photographing birds for some time now and was thrilled when I captured this cute pose. I think he was as interested in me as I was in him.

Ashley Buckler
BETHEL, OHIO

EAT UP
Eastern towhees are not picky eaters. Insects, fruits and berries are on the menu, and seeds are the main course in winter.

This photograph is as much about my journey as it is about the image. On a January morning, after hearing of a snowy owl at Jones Beach State Park off Long Island, New York, I drove several hours from my home in Connecticut. I then spent the better part of two days looking for the owl, without success. As I was making my way back to the parking lot, I passed a bird photographer that I had chatted with several months prior, and shared my tale of disappointment. He said, "Come with me. I know where the snowy hangs out." As promised, a snowy owl perched on the dune greeted us.

Pasquale Finelli NEW HAVEN, CONNECTICUT

We had the good fortune of receiving visits from small flocks of evening grosbeaks in our central Maine yard one winter. On a morning in early January during a snow squall, this beauty did me a favor—it took off directly at me. I was ready with my camera, and it was a thrilling moment!

Pamela Ewing EMBDEN, MAINE

I filled my peanut feeder, and California scrub-jays cleaned it out in one day!

Lornna Nunez
PROSSER, WASHINGTON

During an irruption

one February, I photographed this male common redpoll. I went through 300 pounds of thistle seed in that month alone. It was amazing to watch. Spotting common redpolls can be hit or miss, so I was blessed that winter. They were all such a joy to watch and I anticipate their return every year, even though I may or may not see them. For this photo, I used my Canon EOS 7D Mark II camera paired with a Sigma 150-600 mm contemporary lens. I love how the winterberries mirror his red cap.

Erik Huebler
CHIPPEWA FALLS, WISCONSIN

We hoped

to see a snowy owl during a birding trip to Minnesota last winter, and we were lucky enough to do so. But we didn't expect to see this northern hawk owl, which we spotted atop a dead birch in Gooseberry State Park. What an exciting bonus!

Tom Thweatt
KATY, TEXAS

They are said to be common,

but this was the first time I had ever seen a tufted titmouse in my area. I like how the titmouse landed in a bush with just a few remaining leaves, which match the bird's orange flanks.

Andy Raupp
MONTELLO, WISCONSIN

The day after a snowstorm, I woke to find this crabapple tree full of hungry pine grosbeaks. The sunrise lighting was perfect, but I had to hurry because the golden tones were disappearing rapidly. A beautiful male posed perfectly for me just as the morning glow faded away.

Dave Shaffer SPRINGBROOK, WISCONSIN

BERRY GOOD
Bluebirds rely heavily on fruits and berries during the cooler months. Dogwood, sumac and hackberry are all wintry bluebird faves.

I received an edible birdhouse as a birthday gift from my grandma. As soon as I hung it, I noticed my resident bluebird pair inspecting it, despite already having four nest boxes! I love this moment because they seem to be in deep discussion over whether to love it or list it.

Gretchen Dunham FRANKLIN, TENNESSEE

Winter is one of my favorite times to take bird photos. After it snows I go out and sprinkle birdseed and sunflower seeds to attract juncos, which are very common in my area. I was lucky to get this shot of a dark-eyed junco that landed on the fence in my backyard.

Lori R. Bramble
CAMBRIDGE, MARYLAND

I was so surprised to see this red-shouldered hawk sitting in my yard. It was such an incredibly proud, lovely visitor!

Kristen Flagg
NORWICH, CONNECTICUT

I didn't realize until later that my Christmas tree lights served as the backdrop for this photo of a dark-eyed junco. The photo, which was taken in my yard, is also one of my mother's favorites—she is the one responsible for my love of birds, butterflies and flowers.

Ava Lanes
PARACHUTE, COLORADO

It was the first snowstorm of the year in Dexter, Michigan, with 11 inches of snow. Yet this hairy woodpecker was out pecking for some bugs on the sweetgum tree in our yard.

Judith Dedes
DEXTER, MICHIGAN

Before a rare winter storm in Mississippi, I made this DIY feeder and filled it with homemade suet. Once it started snowing, birds flocked to it, often fighting for a spot to sit and eat. The white-throated sparrow in this photo seems to be saying, "Is there room for me?" as it flies in to find an empty perch. The cardinals, sparrows, juncos, pine warblers and house finches kept me busy filling the feeder multiple times each day.

Penny Rice OAKLAND, MISSISSIPPI

STAY OR GO?

Blue jays have an unusual approach to migration. Some head south when it gets cold while others stay put. And some switch it up from year to year.

I'm someone who would rather be outside when the mercury drops, especially when everything is wonderfully blanketed in snow. The air is crisp and there is a beautiful silence—until a blue jay's raucous call breaks the stillness, alerting other creatures to my presence. I have often called blue jays "the woods patrol."

Doug Dearinger FRANKFORT, KENTUCKY

During winter, the gray color of white-winged doves tends to blend in with the gray skies and tree branches. But on this particular day, the sky was a clear, beautiful blue as this dove sat in a tree. I've always loved the many doves that visit my yard, especially since they symbolize peace.

Julie Risk
GRAPEVINE, TEXAS

While visiting my parents in northern Wisconsin, an early winter storm came and coated everything with ice. I went out with my camera to photograph black-capped chickadees. They did not seem bothered in the least by their icy perches.

Jody Partin
CASTLETON-ON-HUDSON, NEW YORK

A cold front hit our area early, just as the cedar waxwings arrived looking for their favorite fruits. I ventured out in the wind and freezing rain to snap some pictures just in case the weather drove them on. While I was able to capture dozens of adorable shots, this one was my favorite. I imagine the bird looking at the sky and thinking, *This doesn't make foraging any easier!*

Kent Hall BENTON, KENTUCKY

BACKYARD POINTER

Grow berries! These little birds are big berry eaters, able to digest an all-fruit diet for months at a stretch.

Last winter, my husband and I made pine cone, peanut butter and seed feeders with our 4-year-old and hung them in a pine tree near our regular feeder. Within a few minutes, a pair of tufted titmice and a chickadee came to investigate. The juncos found clever ways to eat from the pine cones, hovering in the air while pecking. A male downy woodpecker fed peacefully until a junco came a little too close for comfort. I was able to photograph his reaction, with his normally smooth head of feathers standing on end as he eyed the intruding junco.

Lindsay Hood GARDNERS, PENNSYLVANIA

It was snowing

moments before I noticed this tufted titmouse while looking out my dining room window. The sun was hazy but cast a gentle light, which brought out the colors of the bird.

Debbie Parker
MEDINA, OHIO

For several weeks before Christmas,

we would hear an owl hooting every night. My son and his daughter found it in a tree, but unfortunately it was too dark for them to get a good look. Then, on Christmas Eve afternoon, this magnificent barred owl flew into our yard, landing in a tree near the house. It remained perched and watchful while my granddaughter grabbed her camera and approached, snapping dozens of pictures. After she finally came back in out of the cold, our owl friend flew away. Santa remembers bird lovers, too!

Rosemary Edwards
ST. JOSEPH, MISSOURI

I photographed this pretty house finch from my kitchen window in Virginia during a snow in January. She may not be flashy with brilliant colors, but I love the muted tones of her feathers and softness that the snow cast upon her.

Susan Tucker
CULPEPER, VIRGINIA

For years, we've kept a bird feeder and suet cakes on our back porch, just outside our sliding glass doors, so we can watch the many different birds that come to eat. One winter, this beautiful blue jay let me capture a memorable snapshot.

Noelle Sippel
WEBSTER, NEW YORK

We had a late-winter snowstorm here in the Umpqua Valley in Oregon, and this lovely varied thrush spent a few days taking shelter in our cedar trees.

Barbara Clark ROSEBURG, OREGON

I had always wanted to see cedar waxwings but previously never had any luck, as they're not often spotted in our area. One afternoon, my husband said, "I think your waxwings are out there." I grabbed my Nikon D500 and headed outside in disbelief. Sure enough, a flock of cedar waxwings was feasting on holly berries in my neighbor's yard.

Danna Cable STATESVILLE, NORTH CAROLINA

A sweet little house finch waited on a snowy branch for its turn at the porch feeders.

Tom Hagen
POST FALLS, IDAHO

Just guessing, but I don't think that this female northern cardinal was a very happy camper! I found her one day, sitting on my front porch railing in the midst of snow. I love backyard birds and enjoy learning so much about their behavior by watching and studying them.

Jean Owens
PARIS, TENNESSEE

SEEKING SHELTER
Cardinals often take cover in evergreens during winter. Add a few trees to your yard to offer them a safe haven from the elements.

These friendly fellas showed up on our feeder during a Pacific Northwest snowstorm. One by one, they would fly from our evergreen trees, making room for one another as they indulged in the suet. Their cooperative spirit amazed us!

Liz Dykstra
LYNDEN, WASHINGTON

Braving a winter storm, this white-throated sparrow rested on the railing on my back deck.

Louis Sapienza
CROWNSVILLE, MARYLAND

During an ice storm in February, I spotted this Carolina chickadee perched on the ice-covered branches of a crape myrtle tree in my backyard. Its expression seemed to convey that it was waiting for spring, as was I. This image is special to me because Carolina chickadees were the first visitors to my backyard feeding stations that I established in 2020, and they are now daily visitors. We don't have too many ice or snowstorms in central Virginia, so this harsh weather provided a unique photo opportunity.

Ann Fulcher MIDLOTHIAN, VIRGINIA

TEAMING UP
American robins
switch things up
during winter
by forming large
flocks, putting
aside their usual
spring territorial
behaviors for a bit.

It was a very cold winter day at only 3 degrees when I took this photo in northern New Hampshire, within a mile of the Canadian border. The robin seemed to be happy while feasting on the abundance of mountain ash berries.

Paul Blossom BRAINTREE, VERMONT

During one of the coldest winters we had experienced recently we were more or less shut in because of heavy snow cover. I walked outside one day and saw these birds sitting pretty on an old clothesline post. From left are a male and female northern cardinal, a purple finch and a dark-eyed junco.

Kay Craig Spurlock
WILMAR, ARKANSAS

I have several feeders and see many kinds of birds all winter. One day the resident blue jays were quite agitated and very vocal. Upon investigation, I found this little boreal owl roosting in a dead tree. It must have decided no sleep was to be had, so it flew off—but not before I got this photo.

Janine Lynch
HUNTSVILLE, ONTARIO

We're very fortunate to have a favored wintering spot for short-eared owls nearby. I went out in a bit of snow, hoping to see one. Bingo!

Linda Keister
LEROY, NEW YORK

I met up with a birding friend who took me to a nature area. One of the first birds we saw was this gorgeous golden-crowned kinglet. They are fun to watch, but they're fast!

Laura Frazier
KEARNEYSVILLE,
WEST VIRGINIA

Every year we share Christmas with the birds by putting our tree out on the deck and filling it with peanuts, birdseed and peanut butter all winter long. I'll bet this blue jay was especially excited about the peanuts!

Caryl Clemens GLADSTONE, MICHIGAN

We have deep snowfalls here in the Cascade Range, and our birds have to be creative to remain healthy and fed. A blue spruce tree provides wonderful cover, and I scatter seeds on the branches. This offers me an optimal area to study bird behaviors and to take photos. I call this image *The March of the California Quails.*

Douglas Beall CAMP SHERMAN, OREGON

I was fortunate to come across this red-tailed hawk in a tree over the parking lot of my local nature center in Fountain, Colorado, where it patiently posed for me.

David Kaley COLORADO SPRINGS, COLORADO

When I wanted to try out my new camera, the female red-bellied woodpecker that frequents our feeders was very cooperative. She gracefully drank from our heated birdbath, and I was thrilled to capture the moment.

Joyce Sorensen
CLEAR LAKE, IOWA

This chestnut-backed chickadee

rested comfortably in an apple tree for a bit before flying to the feeder. It was a great snapshot opportunity.

Dan Garber
TROY, MONTANA

TINY ONES

Chestnut-backed chickadees, found year-round in the Pacific Northwest, are slightly smaller than their more common black-capped and Carolina cousins.

I took this photo of a **stunning** male northern flicker off my back deck during a brutally cold January morning. I had been waiting for him to come by all morning, and then he struck just the right pose! I was very pleased with the outcome, and it remains a favorite photo of mine.

Rick Rauzi
ALTOONA, IOWA

For several days in January, temperatures lingered around 20 below zero, and an extraordinary number of redpolls frequented our thistle feeder. This particular female was reluctant to leave the feeder. She would just fluff up her feathers, tuck her head in and sleep right there. I think she didn't want to lose her spot.

Dawn Glass
RED LAKE FALLS,
MINNESOTA

On a stormy February afternoon, our neighbor called to say he had an owl in his fireplace that needed rescuing, and to ask if we had a net. We own cockatiels, so we know something about handling birds. My husband, Mark, grabbed a pair of thick leather gloves and headed next door.

The little eastern screech-owl was scared, but when Mark put out his hand, it hopped right on. When he walked the owl outside, Mark said he could feel the talons through the leather gloves. The beautiful bird flew up to our downspout and rested after its ordeal, then flew away to enjoy life as a free bird.

Noreen Schuster VIRGINIA BEACH, VIRGINIA

It does not snow often where I live, but my backyard got about 2 inches before the sun was ready to come out. So I quickly ran outside with my Nikon D750 camera and Tamron SP 150-600 mm lens. My hands were really cold, but when I saw this male eastern bluebird land on a tree filled with snow and ice I had to photograph him. I call this photo *My Winter Bluebird*.

Marilyn Diaz FUQUAY-VARINA, NORTH CAROLINA

I was playing around with my camera, shooting this male red-bellied woodpecker, when a yellow flash came out of nowhere. We don't often see northern flickers, and here a male flew right into my photo! As he sent the red-bellied flying away, I held down the shutter for a burst of photos. I couldn't believe my eyes when I saw all the brilliant gold under his wings and tail feathers.

Jeffrey Hunt
WINDSOR, CONNECTICUT

This little dark-eyed junco lingered at the feeder for some time after its meal. Perhaps it welcomed the sunlight's warmth. I certainly welcomed the opportunity for a close-up!

Richard Cox
BUMPASS, VIRGINIA

My husband and I enjoy watching the cardinal couples that visit our backyard. They like to hang out in our white birch trees near the feeders. I had been trying to get a good picture of Papa Cardinal, as we like to call him. On this day, Papa C. landed in the birch tree, and there was a tiny opening in the snowy branches that I could focus my camera through.

Patty Weik
FREEPORT, ILLINOIS

Each winter

we fill a wine barrel with winterberry branches and berry-bearing cedar sprigs, then wait for the bluebirds. They usually do not disappoint us. They bring color to an otherwise drab time of year and give us so much pleasure as we watch them. They have graced our warm birdbath and berry barrel for many years.

Marie & Richard Nieber
NORTHBOROUGH, MASSACHUSETTS

A year-round resident of the aspen groves in the ravine behind our cabin in the Rocky Mountains, this red-shafted northern flicker adds a welcome flash of color to our white winters.

Carmel Mawle RED FEATHER LAKES, COLORADO

Although house finches are common here in northern Indiana, I consider them far from ordinary. This female may not have the rosy color the male has, but her brown and gray stripes are simply beautiful. Perched on a branch with snow and red berries, she posed for a very pretty picture.

Ted Rose NORTH MANCHESTER, INDIANA

I rarely have a chance to get a shot of Gambel's quail because they're so shy and quick. However, after a crazy snowfall in Chino Valley, Arizona, these little guys were in my tree hoping I would put out seeds. I finally got my photo of them, at long last.

Catherine Fillebrown
CHINO VALLEY, ARIZONA

For years we've put a feeder and suet right outside our sliding glass doors so we can catch glimpses of the many different birds that come by to eat, especially in winter. One of my favorites was this friendly tufted titmouse, just hanging out in the snow and wind.

Noelle Sippel
WEBSTER, NEW YORK

With a heavy blanket, tripod, Canon SLR camera and hot cocoa, I'll layer up, open my sliding glass door and wait by the feeders for a photo. We had a terrible blizzard one January, and I shot hundreds of photos until it was too dark. I got some amazing lineups on the fence.

Carol Estes
LA PORTE, INDIANA

Short-eared owls were hunting in a field near my home. Checking them out, I saw this one at the side of the road. Every time a car went by, the owl flattened out like this, as if challenging the car! It was exciting to watch.

Jane Miller
PENFIELD, NEW YORK

BIG RANGE
Short-eared owls are found from the Americas to Europe, Asia and even many oceanic islands.

For a few years, we have had a pair of Anna's hummingbirds sticking around over winter, even through the snow. We keep our hummingbird feeder in an insulated box with a lightbulb (my stepfather's idea) to keep the liquid from freezing. I've learned that a steady diet of insects helps sustain them through the cold months, too.

Sarah Lindquist PORT ANGELES, WASHINGTON

We had an early November snowstorm in Michigan. The birds are very active when it snows, so I always have my camera nearby. When I looked out my back window, I saw this beautiful mourning dove sitting on the deck rail.

Natalie McCloy CLARKSTON, MICHIGAN

Our Anna's hummingbirds

didn't seem to mind the falling snow, but they did move their lookout under our patio roof. It doesn't snow very often in these parts, so this was probably something completely new to them.

Rick Williams
TUCSON, ARIZONA

DID YOU KNOW?

Most North American hummingbirds migrate, but some Anna's hummingbirds remain year-round in one area.

I waited patiently for more than an hour at the park to get just the right image of this merlin perched high in a tree. My patience paid off with this photo and many others. I call this one *Defiant* because the pose looks just that way to me.

Ray Mueller
BEAVERCREEK, OHIO

Cold-Weather Warriors

Known for nomadic movements, bold feather patterns and special adaptations for surviving chilly temps, these birds brave frigid, snowy conditions and delight bird-watchers across the country.

By Lisa Ballard

JOHANN SCHUMACHER DESIGN

Snowy owls are usually seen in open areas such as fields and coastlines.

Snowy Owls

Snowy owls sport striking white plumage and piercing yellow eyes. They are true dwellers of the Arctic, where lemmings are their favorite food. Snowies hunt any time of day during the summer. They are the heaviest owl in North America at about 4 pounds, and their thick feathers insulate them from the cold. They show up during the winter around the Great Lakes, northern New England and the north-central plains, sometimes in considerable numbers, looking for prey.

"These periodic irruptions are not, as widely assumed, caused by a lack of prey in the Arctic, but the reverse," says Scott Weidensaul, ornithologist and co-founder of Project SNOWstorm, which specifically studies snowy owls. "When there's a productive breeding season in the North, itself a result of a boom in lemming populations, all those young owls making their first migration south produce the periodic invasions. Far from being desperate and starving, most of them are perfectly healthy."

White-winged and Red Crossbills

Crossbills, common across Canada and western boreal regions, are best known for their twisted beaks, the tips of which don't match up. With these unique crossed bills, they pry open conifer cones to get the nutritious seeds inside. When food is plentiful, crossbills breed, even during the winter. If there are no cones, they irrupt, sometimes coming to feeders stuffed with sunflower seeds.

"Crossbills will feed when there's 3 feet of snow on the ground, but if the snow is heavy and wet or there's an ice storm, they'll move," says Matt Young, founder and president of the Finch Research Network. "They only come to feeders as a last resort and usually in late winter or early spring when wild food is limited."

4 Cool Bird Facts

- Hummingbirds can drop their internal temperature, inducing a temporary state of torpor, which means they need less energy, and less food, to withstand frigid temperatures.

- Like people, birds shiver to stay warm. When they shiver, their muscles create heat.

- By preening and fluffing feathers, birds create an insulating layer and outer jacket to shield themselves from weather. Fluffing creates pockets of warm air around their bodies. Preening spreads a protective oil and locks together their outer feathers, making them weatherproof.

- Some birds, such as crows, huddle on dense shrubs and evergreens to share body warmth. Cavity nesters, such as nuthatches and titmice, cuddle inside tree cavities.

White-winged crossbill

Snow buntings form flocks in the hundreds during winter.

Snow Buntings

Snow buntings breed above the Arctic Circle and are the northernmost songbirds. Males arrive in spring about a month ahead of females, withstanding subzero temperatures to claim a nest site among the cold rocks. Once the females lay their eggs, males deliver food so their mates can stay in the nest most of the time.

During the winter, snow buntings head as far south as the central United States, where you might spot them as they flit from field to field. "There isn't much for trees where snow buntings come from, so they feed where they can access the ground," says Melissa Mayntz, author of *Migration: Exploring the Remarkable Journeys of Birds*. "When I lived in Utah, I would throw seeds under a table on our patio. The snow buntings would quickly figure out, 'food!' They like mixed seeds, millet and black oil sunflower seeds."

As one of their winter survival strategies, snow buntings don't molt twice as do most birds. In spring, their worn-down feathers reveal new ones. What's more, their feather density is higher to prevent heat loss, especially at the base of their bills and on their lower legs. They will also fly or flop into snowdrifts, making a little hollow to stay warm.

Bohemian Waxwings

Bohemian waxwings are another northern breeder, in this case from
Alaska to Hudson Bay. But during the winter they wander like black-
masked vagabonds across the northwestern United States and western
Canada in search of fruits and berries. They also irregularly drift into
New England, the northern Midwest and Ontario.

"Bohemian waxwings are unpredictable, suddenly appearing and then
leaving. They fly to the best food source, strip it clean, then move on,"
Melissa says. "They travel in large groups, following the leader to find
the best feeding spots. If you plant fruit trees, such as crabapples or
even junipers, and leave the fruit, the odds are high they'll find them."

**Bohemian
waxwings
travel south in
winter looking
for fruit trees.**

JOHN GILL

Lapland Longspurs

After breeding on the Arctic tundra, Lapland longspurs form large nomadic flocks during the winter—sometimes groups consist of more than a million birds! The chunky songbirds forage for seeds to eat in patches of low grass and vegetation and on bare ground, especially on agricultural lands and coastal dunes.

"Lapland longspurs will flock with highly social snow buntings," Melissa says. "Both species are ground feeders and have similar food preferences and behaviors."

Lapland longspur

BOB KOTHENBEUTEL

Evening Grosbeaks

These hulking finches, with conical bills and striking yellow forehead patches and chests on males, are like a burst of sunshine when they visit feeders. Evening grosbeaks breed in the North and West but migrate south during winter as far as they need to for food. They love sunflower seeds, though the planting of ornamental box elders is credited with their spread across the northeastern and mid-Atlantic states.

"Evening grosbeaks irrupt farther south during the winter when there are food shortages and to escape inclement weather," Matt says. "They like platform or hopper feeders, because they travel in large, gregarious flocks and have voracious appetites, hence their nicknames 'gross-pigs' or 'grocery-beaks.'"

Evening grosbeak

Gray-crowned rosy-finches enjoy dining on sunflower seeds scattered on the ground or from platform feeders.

Rosy-Finches

Three species of rosy-finches are closely related: black, gray-crowned and brown-capped. Black and brown-capped rosy-finches are among the highest-elevation breeding birds in North America, often nesting above 14,000 feet. They roost together for protection, often in conifers.

"They'll stay as long as they can up high until they run out of food, then they'll move lower to protected valleys. A few hundred feet can mean the difference between a snowstorm and no snow. Or they'll go to the leeward side of a hill," Matt says. "They're attracted to weed fields in the winter for seeds, but they'll come to a feeder filled with sunflower or Nyjer seeds."

FROM TOP: STEVE AND DAVE MASLOWSKI; PAUL BANNICK

Common redpoll

BRIAN ZWIEBEL

Hoary and Common Redpolls

Common redpolls, with their red chests and red caps, and their paler cousins, hoary redpolls, withstand winter's extremes by tunneling into the snow to stay warm during the night. "Redpolls are the most northern of the finches. They even bathe in the snow!" Matt says.

To feed, redpolls seek out tiny seeds from birch, alder, conifers and many other plants, gathering them into their throat pouches and flying to a more protected spot to eat. In winter, they can ingest 40% of their weight in seed a day.

By putting on about 30% more feathers during the winter, these residents of the Arctic and northernmost boreal forests can survive -65 degrees, but they will migrate as far south as the central United States, congregating at feeders. "They'll eat sunflower seeds, but they love thistle and Nyjer," Matt says.

6 Winter Bird Hot Spots

Get out your binoculars.
A birding paradise might be
a lot closer than you think.

By Jill Staake

Merritt Island National Wildlife Refuge, Titusville, Florida

Special sightings: roseate spoonbill, reddish egret, Florida scrub-jay

Situated a few miles south of the Kennedy Space Center, Merritt Island is one of central Florida's best winter birding spots. An array of migratory waterfowl flock here in the thousands, which offers visitors chances to see hooded mergansers, northern pintails and many more.

Regular residents include some of Florida's best species such as the roseate spoonbill—and alligator sightings are pretty much guaranteed. Take the 7-mile Black Point Wildlife Drive through saltwater marsh and pine flatwoods for easy viewing of the refuge's most fascinating creatures. Look for songbirds and raptors while hiking the Cruickshank Trail, and scan the roadsides toward Canaveral National Seashore for your best chance to see scrub-jays.

Merritt Island
National Wildlife
Refuge

San Pedro Riparian National Conservation Area, Hereford, Arizona

Special sightings: ferruginous hawk, golden eagle, pyrrhuloxia

Southeast Arizona is one of the most biologically diverse areas in the United States. Deserts, canyons and isolated mountain ranges known as sky islands provide habitats for hundreds of avian species throughout the year.

Trails that start at San Pedro House, a historic estate in the park, route along the river through cottonwood forest, where you'll spot specialties such as the Gila woodpecker, black phoebe and Abert's towhee. In desert areas, look for curve-billed thrashers and wintering flocks of lark buntings.

Drive less than an hour east to the Whitewater Draw Wildlife Area to see a massive gathering of more than 20,000 wintering sandhill cranes, along with other wading birds and waterfowl. Ferruginous hawks, the largest hawks in the U.S., are found here, too.

The namesake river flows through San Pedro Riparian National Conservation Area.

Left: The canopy walk offers a close view of Santa Ana National Wildlife Refuge treetops. Below: A green jay in South Texas.

Santa Ana National Wildlife Refuge and Bentsen-Rio Grande Valley State Park, Hidalgo County, Texas

Special sightings: green jay, plain chachalaca, hook-billed kite

Spot Central American fliers without needing a passport in this Texas hot spot just north of the Mexican border. Late winter and early spring are prime birding seasons here, with very mild temperatures and abundant wildlife.

The feeders outside the Santa Ana National Wildlife Refuge visitor center attract southern favorites such as Altamira orioles and golden-fronted woodpeckers. Hike the lake trails to see three types of kingfishers (green, belted and ringed) and plenty of other water lovers.

Twenty miles west, Bentsen-Rio Grande Valley State Park offers a two-story wheelchair-accessible Hawk Observation Tower to give you a true bird's-eye view. Don't miss the nearby National Butterfly Center, where plantings have attracted more than 230 butterfly species, including rare tropical visitors.

Klamath Basin, Northern California and Southern Oregon

Special sightings: Barrow's goldeneye, bald eagle, white-headed woodpecker

The Klamath Basin is a major layover on the famed Pacific Flyway. Multiple freshwater habitats—including lakes, rivers and marshes—attract wading birds and waterfowl in unbelievable numbers.

Snow geese, cackling geese and Ross's geese are winter regulars, along with Clark's grebes and common and Barrow's goldeneyes. More than 500 bald eagles, the largest concentration in the continental U.S., spend winter around the Klamath Basin. Combine a drive along the 10-mile Lower Klamath National Wildlife Refuge Auto Tour Route marshes with a trip to Lava Beds National Monument's upland habitat to maximize the diversity of your sightings.

Snow geese at Klamath Basin

A photographer at Cape Henlopen State Park

Cape Henlopen State Park and Delaware Seashore State Park, Sussex County, Delaware

Special sightings: snow bunting, long-tailed duck, razorbill

Delaware's Cape Henlopen State Park offers views of both Delaware Bay and the Atlantic Ocean and is a haven for wintering geese, ducks and other waterbirds. You'll find all three types of scoter here, alongside diving seabirds such as northern gannets. Look closely at flocks of double-crested cormorants, as great cormorants often mingle with them. Scan the dunes for snow buntings or even the rare Lapland longspur.

Nearby Delaware Seashore State Park's Indian River Inlet is another excellent location where you might spot pelagic species such as razorbills, dovekies or murres.

Niagara Falls,
along the Niagara
Birding Trail

ANDREIORLOV/GETTY IMAGES

The Niagara Birding Trail, Niagara and Erie County, New York

Special sightings: Iceland gull, peregrine falcon, harlequin duck

The entire Niagara River Corridor, which includes Niagara Falls and the Niagara Birding Trail, is a popular tourist destination and a special place for winter birders. Gathering here in multitudes are gulls and waterfowl, including many that breed in the far northern Arctic, such as Iceland gulls and tundra swans.

Areas directly surrounding the falls, including Goat Island, are ideal places to look for up to a dozen species of gull, with the possibility of rare visitors such as black-headed gull. Woodpeckers, nuthatches and titmice abound at feeders and along wooded trails on the Dufferin Islands, offering a tranquil break from the busy falls area.